Cousin Tyr was an atlatl expert

Cousin Tyr
A Proud Meskwaki

Dwain L. Kitchel, Sr.

TENNESSEE VALLEY
Publishing®

Knoxville, Tennessee
2023

 This is a work of fiction wrapped and bound with historical facts.

Published by Tennessee Valley Publishing
5320 Yosemite Trail
Knoxville, Tennessee 37909

Printed, bound, and graphic designs by Graphic Creations, Knoxville, TN.

For information about Meskwaki couple on the cover, see the image of Captured Meskwakis and Others on page 186.

ISBN 1-932604-88-X

Dedicated to the memory of

Margaret Cockman Kitchel

Margaret knew America's greatest crimes were committed against our Native American cousins.

Today, DNA analysis, archaeological evidence, and most major religions agree: All human beings are cousins.

Yes, we are all related!

an old man[1]

I sang
to the warm sun
and cold moon
this morning
and offered
myself
to the land
and gods
for them
to
teach
me
the old
hard tests of living
all over again

Ray Young Bear
Meskwaki Poet Laureate

---

[1] Open Road, Integrated Media Inc., New York, NY 10014 from *Manifestation Wolverine, The Collected Poetry of Ray Young Bear,* published 2015.

Contents

Contents (Continued)

List of Illustrations and Photographs

The 2022 Meskwaki photographs are printed courtesy of the Meskwaki Nation.

Preface

This story began as an attempt to strengthen the belief that blue-eyed Vikings were the *first to mate with dark-eyed Native American females*. Two ancient Icelandic sagas, the Saga of the Greenlanders and the Saga of Erik the Red, were major factors in this guess.

In 1960, the Norwegian explorer Helge Ingstad and his wife, Anne Stine Ingstad, made a historic discovery at the northern tip of Canada's Newfoundland. They found an 11th-century Viking settlement near a small village named L'Anse aux Meadows. Because of land described in the Icelandic sagas, the Ingstads named the site Vinland.

To document a clear path between Vikings and early blue-eyed Native Americans, tribes first encountered must be linked to later tribes. Geographically and time-wise, the **Meskwaki Tribe** (sometimes spelled "Mesquakie") was an excellent link option.

As Meskwaki Tribe research unfolded, blue eyes from the Vikings became a minor story compared to the centuries of unbelievable hardships faced and bravely handled by the Meskwaki people. Their story of heroic achievement against gigantic odds is a compelling and continuing **Saga**. The Vikings were relegated to Appendix B in this book.

The precise location of the earliest Meskwaki Tribe is unknown. In 1614, they were located in the St. Lawrence River Valley north of present-day Ontario, Canada. The Meskwaki Tribe's largest population estimates usually range between 2,500 and 20,000.

Face-to-face, the Meskwakis fought the French and powerful Chippewa and Sioux tribes. At some point the Meskwakis had to be a large tribe, almost certainly much larger than 2,500.

The first documented Meskwaki contact with the French was in 1665. After the 1730 massacre near present-day Arrowsmith, Illinois, the French, with help from their friendly Algonquin tribes, had reduced Meskwakis to about 400 living souls. Chief Kiala was the Meskwaki's leader. They established a new village on the Wisconsin River in modern day Richland County, Wisconsin. By 1732, attacks by French allied tribes on the weakened Meskwakis wounded Chief Kiala and reduced the Meskwaki population to about 50 warriors and 90 women and children. This was when **Meskwaki's saga** almost ceased to exist!

Whatever the estimated counts, thousands of Meskwakis lost their lives during this approximately 67 years. Most were killed by arrows, spears, musket balls, tomahawks, hatchets, knives, intentional fires, and European diseases.

Meskwaki notoriety as great warriors and success in interfering with France's effort to ship raw materials from North America caused the tribe to receive an enormous amount of European-colonialism written information. Today, that makes it easier to find Meskwaki information from their deep past.

To help understand their culture, customs, and living conditions that spawned the success of present-day Meskwakis now residing in Tama, Iowa, it was decided to try and walk or canoe about 4,000 miles in Cousin Tyr's moccasins. **Of course, this is impossible!** Fortunately, *trying to reconstruct the story* is possible. Here, we will use their Meskwaki name throughout; not Fox, which was both a French and American mistake.

Cousin Tyr lived in the chaotic years from 1700 to 1788. A time when America, the greatest melting pot the world has ever known, emerged from the chaos and ashes. The chaos included relocating or killing millions of Native Americans.

Acknowledgments

Elizabeth Kitchel Ethridge and David Laurence Kitchel proofread several draft versions of this manuscript. Elizabeth is an outstanding proofreader and was a tremendous help in the cover design. David is a poet and bookworm for a wide range of subject matter. They corrected a number of missteps. **Thank you, Elizabeth and David.**

When personal friend, Ely Yang, learned of this book project, he became interested, and helped drive from Knoxville, Tennessee to Wisconsin, where we visited Prairie du Chien and spent several days driving up and down Wisconsin Highway 131, which, like a shadow, follows the beautiful and crooked Kickapoo River. We found the location of Cousin Tyr's childhood village. **Thank you, Ely**.

Jonathan Buffalo, is a long-time distinguished Meskwaki Historian and now their Historical Preservation Director. His work was used to confirm much of the information gathered from other sources and his words directly used in large sections of the Epilogue. I join Meskwaki citizens and countless others who are indebted to this gentleman, whom I never had the privilege of personally meeting. **Thank you, Mr. Buffalo**.

For Meskwaki history and current activities, a trip to the Meskwaki website https://www.meskwaki.org is highly recommended. Even better, if possible, is a visit to their Tama, Iowa, attractions and facilities.

Prologue

By 1500 A.D., when many Europeans began arriving, more than 500 Native American tribes were scattered across North America. Estimates of the tribes' total population range from one million to eighteen million. Scholarly attempts to reconcile these estimates typically report about five to 10 million Native Americans lived north of the Rio Grande River. As this disparity shows, no one knows a precise estimate.

From 1500 A.D. until America's Revolutionary War, Native Americans were continually pressured by the British, French, Dutch, and Spanish governments and immigrants from these countries. It was a dangerous time, especially for Native Americans. For more than 60 years, Meskwakis had resisted French encroachment and turned deaf ears to France's Jesuit priests.

The French began using a river on land occupied by the Meskwakis, who lived there long before the French learned the river was an important connection to the Mississippi River. Despite repeated Meskwaki warnings, the French kept using the river to provide guns to Meskwaki's western enemy—the Sioux.

Meskwakis killed a number of French trespassers. ***Interference with France's commerce was the Meskwakis cardinal sin!*** This led to ***France's effort to exterminate the Meskwaki people.***[1]

No policy against Native Americans exceeded the overt horror of total extermination. Cousin Tyr, a proud and loyal Meskwaki, helped fight the French and was among the few who survived the attempted genocide.

---

[1]King Louis XV ordered the genocide. Ironically, the King was only 18 years old and was known as the Beloved. Archbishop Cardinal de Fleury signed orders for him.

During 1750 the colonial population of America was about one million while New France's population was about 10 percent of the million. Surprisingly, New France controlled about twice the area of other European invaders combined. The illustration below

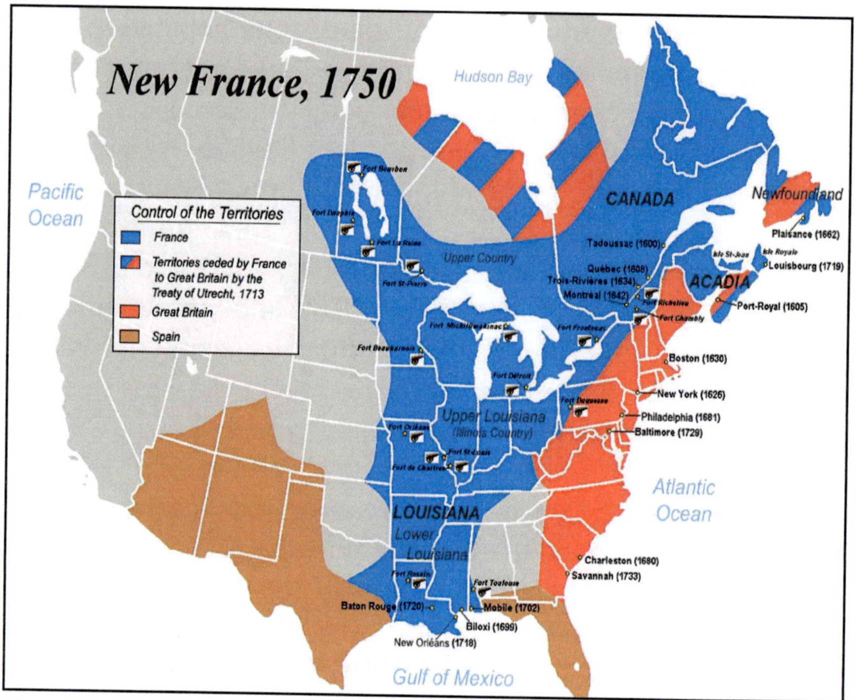

New France's domain reached from northeast Canada to the Gulf of Mexico. The Mississippi River provided France with a direct path from the important Great Lakes area to the Gulf of Mexico.
This map was furnished courtesy of Wikimedia Common's user Karl Musser.

shows New France's territorial dominance. Cousin Tyr's existence was a microscopic sliver of this dangerous era. When the Revolutionary War ended in 1783, America's immigrant population was three million, while aggression, guns, and diseases reduced the Native American people to about one million. These Native Americans now had a new problem: A focused and vicious aggressor— **the United States of America.**

Introduction by Tyr

The keen eyes of a soaring eagle watched the morning sun glisten off the Kickapoo River far below. I've seen it glitter many times from neighboring bluffs. It's a crooked thread stretching and meandering across the land like it was stitched there by a confused Wisaka—the eldest son of Kehci Manitou.[2]

Zigzagging the Kickapoo bends, loops, and snakes back and forth as it seeks a southern direction to the Wisconsin River. As a boy, it was my playground, provider, escape, and more.

If the eagle climbed a little higher, it could see 100 miles in any direction. Several times this distance held me captive for the first 17 winters of my life. The distance caged this body. Nevertheless, it didn't interfere with an active imagination frequently ignited by my Uncle Leno.

Once, he announced, "The Kickapoo is a lot like life, going here and there, sometimes serene, sometimes wild, sometimes giving, and sometimes taking. The Kickapoo and life constantly change by forces we can't fully know or control."

At the time, I was about 10 winters old and we were on a high bluff watching a muddy, violent Kickapoo cover over and rip away our crops of corn, beans, and squash. Then his words were just words. I could only think about our food being washed away. My worried response was, "*What will we eat?*"

With his voice of authority, Uncle Leno calmly explained, "The Kickapoo, by its flooding marks, showed it

---

[2] Kehci Manitou is the Meskwaki's closest expression for the God of many cultures. It means the Greatest Spirit residing among the stars. Various spellings include Kitche and others. Wisaka, his eldest son, created Earth and everything on or in it.

hadn't flooded this high before, so we guessed our fields would be safe. We guessed wrong! We made another guess that someday it might flood higher, therefore we placed the village and stored plenty of food and seeds on higher ground. Don't worry Tyr; we will replant and survive this angry flood. We can't know the future, so we have to guess."

Uncle Leno was a wise man. The unknown surrounds our past and present and lurks ahead of us, no matter who, when, or where we are. *Therefore, we all make a lot of wrong guesses*!

Now I am an old man who never guessed my words would be written on paper. Yet, here I am with my loving great-granddaughter, Grace Elyshia Doyle. Grace wants to preserve a few of my memories of family, friends, beliefs, living conditions, activities, and adventures. She believes some of our descendants might appreciate these words.

Tyr,

Meskwaki Hunter,
Defensive Warrior,
and Bag-of-Bones

An overview of a section of the Kickapoo River that illustrates how crooked the river still is. The Kickapoo is among the several most crooked rivers in America.

This photograph was furnished courtesy of the Village of Gays Mills, WI 54631.

Grace Elyshia Doyle Questions for her Great-grandfather Tyr (St. Louis Settlement, October 1786)

How old are you?

Not sure, probably about 90 winters. I've seen so many winters that most people from my youth have gone to their respective rewards, leaving me to endure the stings of old age. Now I lay around like an old dog gumming clabbered milk between naps. My greatest joys and saddest moments are thinking and talking about the past. My earthly future is destined to be a burden to others, but past events have drained my tears. These eyes have no tears left for being a burden.

Speaking of eyes, why do you have blue eyes?

Not sure. Grandfather Nodin told us, "Long before the French began taking our beavers, a few of our early ancestors were pale men with blue eyes." Grandfather Nodin was a truth talker.

Can you describe the villages of your youth?

Yes! I spent my youth in one village on the Kickapoo River. See the knife marks on my black panther walking cane? The cane shaft came from an early atlatl spear. Each mark means something to me. Like you rereading pages from your diary, I've rubbed my fingers over these cuts many times, revisting early memories.

What was your favorite adventure?

It was a canoe trip down and back up the Mississippi River.

§§§

Tyr Comments

Unable to read or write any language, I am pleased that Grace will write these words. Written words survive while ancestors' talk fades like shouts bouncing off mountain walls. Written words are better reflections. Sadly, they can be lies or mistakes as well as the truth. Our aim will be at the truth, realizing truth is a tricky word tortured by time and twisted and tainted by the past of both talkers and listeners.

For this talker, it's important English words are used rather than French. I can't read, write, or speak either. The French, with their muskets in one hand and religious crosses in the other, tried to kill or sell as slaves every Meskwaki; including our women and children. They had far more success killing us than their black-robe Jesuits did, attempting to change our beliefs and culture.

Sure, there are good French people. I met some. Regardless, I can't let go of hatred for the scheming, murdering Frenchmen! Their actions, directly, and indirectly, killed many thousands (almost all) of our independent and proud people.

There is no question that our intense Meskwaki warriors showed little mercy toward enemies and believed a fair fight was one Meskwaki versus two enemies.

Sometimes I can't remember why I went from one place to the next. Still, my head holds many early memories, and each memory begets others.

Answers to Grace's questions can spread lots of ink. The words put in the mouths of other talkers cannot be exact. Yet, they represent people and experiences clearly recalled.

§§§

Early Memories

Happy Little Village on the Kickapoo River

According to my mother, Anna, our family, with several other families fleeing French exploitation and tribal adversaries, started our happy little village on the banks of the Kickapoo River. This was six winters before I was born. Anna kept a cedar post where she whittled information concerning births and events with cuts only she fully understood. She had the post dug up and moved with us when later our village was moved farther down the Kickapoo.

My earliest vivid memory occurred during spring when I was about three winters old and playing with sister Alawa, who was three winters older. She ordered your talker to bring her small rocks from the nearby woods to outline the walls of a play lodge.

When picking up a rock, to my great surprise, a squeezed-flat flower appeared. Slowly it began to unfurl and open toward the morning sun. With its stem and petals reaching out and inhaling the sunbeams, the flower was small, fragile, and beautiful. It captured my young mind. Even now, I can close my eyes and see the delicate shades of blue and purple with a tiny, yellow, and hairy eye staring at the sun. Later, I learned the flower was called a violet.

It's strange what insignificant events we remember with clarity and perhaps stranger the number of important events that evaporate from or remain hidden inside one's head.

Our Kickapoo River was guarded by oak, hickory, cedar, aspen, ginkgo, maple, birch, pine, and other trees. There was fertile land for crops of corn, squash, melons, pumpkins, beans, and tobacco. Abundant game was close and included buffalo, bear, elk, deer, beaver, turkey, and smaller animals and birds. Berries, nuts, and useful plants surrounded us. We kept a lot of dogs handy to warn of approaching strangers—man or beast. The dogs were well fed because they filled our pots as the main ingredient in a delicious stew served on special occasions.

The Kickapoo, its feeder streams, and the nearby Wisconsin and Mississippi Rivers provided us with water, fish, crawdads, mussels, frogs, and turtles. Daily we used one or more of these rivers or streams for drinking, cooking, cleaning, transportation, and recreation.

Icy-cold springs directly fed the Kickapoo River and its other feeder streams. This kept the Kickapoo cooler in the summer. The temperature of all the springs' water stayed constant in the winter, keeping the Kickapoo warm enough it rarely froze over. This helped make our area liveable year around. Unlike many, we didn't move about because of winter weather. Our winters weren't mild and we had plenty of cold, sleet, and snow. Snowshoes were a necessity.

Once, I wondered out loud to Uncle Leno about there being so many springs, creeks, and rivers. He answered, "Tyr, you have no idea how big the land is or how many springs, creeks, and rivers lace it together. Wisaka made streams more plentiful than people." I said nothing, but opened my eyes wider and tilted my head in disbelief.

Raising his voice because of my body language, he continued, "The springs, creeks, and rivers supply water to quench the thirst of people, animals, and anything else living like grass and trees. They also help fill the lakes and seas." He paused. Then in a lower tone said, "With the help of Grandfather Sun, the running water along with lakes and seas make the clouds. Winds spread the clouds and water over the earth's surface." Often, Uncle Leno backed his pronouncements with powerful words listeners couldn't disprove.

Silently, I counted no more than 20 creeks or feeder streams and approximately 50 springs and believed there were at least 300 people living on our short, crooked Kickapoo River. Despite my count disagreeing with Uncle Leno's proclamation, challenging an elder's explanation wasn't the Meskwaki way. Shaking my head in agreement, I muttered something like, "Oh, I see." Besides, I had no idea how many rivers were under us. In deep caves, water flowed and cold springs kept bubbling up in new places; maybe Uncle Leno was correct.

There's little wonder why our village was a happy place for youngsters. Here elders answered questions and nurtured us to be proud of our heritage. Here they shielded the young from troubles outside our cocoon of happiness. As we grew older, they taught us with words and actions (not punishments) the importance of hard work, being kind to others, and defending rights against those who threatened our way of life or dishonored our family, clan, or tribe.

Youngsters didn't sass their parents or elders. Why? Not sure, except we honored them. It was okay to grumble outside their hearing and disobey a few rules, but not directly question their wisdom or authority. Besides, I knew they knew more than me.

Meskwakis were taught that we are special. Wisaka molded us, *the first people*, from Earth's red clay and named us the Red Earth people. Meskwaki means the Red Earth People! Earthly death for everyone is as natural as life. While feeling bad about earthly death, it had to be accepted as well as life.

We were taught there were spirits called manitous. They are everywhere and in everything. They are with people, the stars, the Earth, animals, trees, plants, and insects. If you can name or think it, it has a manitou. A few are great and powerful, some weak, some friendly, and some evil. Even rocks have manitous. When we heat a rock with fire to use in our sweat lodge, its manitou comes to the surface. By splashing water on the heated rock, it's manitou combines with the surrounding air, fire, and water manitous. This causes our bodies to sweat, driving out poison and pain. This makes us feel better. We've done it often, so it must be true. There may be other guesses for this miracle. None makes more sense to a Meskwaki than manitous.

Kehci Manitou, the greatest manitou, dwells on the banks of the White River of stars (Milky Way). Other stars shining there were once special manitous on Earth. An ordinary manitou, like mine, doesn't go there. When our body dies, its manitou remains in its earthly home four days before traveling toward the Happy Hunting Ground. This spirit world is due west beyond the setting sun. Our manitous must cross a wiggling bridge capable of shaking evil manitous into the river of manitou death and the domain of Machi Manitou (the evil spirit). When successful manitous arrive at their new home, they find a pleasant place filled with endless pleasures like playing games, dancing, feasting, and resting.

Earthly death doesn't end our manitous, it just propels our spirits toward the Happy Hunting Ground. Defending honor, being kind, and helping others, make crossing the wiggling bridge easy.

We were taught to think for ourselves. We needed to follow village rules, although it was okay to question spiritual issues. Most of us were too busy to worry much about such matters and readily accepted the wisdom of our elders concerning the existence of manitous and the Happy Hunting Ground.

Meskwaki and other tribes have differing views of the spiritual world, as do the white people. To my knowledge, none of our tribes killed each other because of these differences. White people's histories are full of stories of millions being killed over religious belief disputes. Our elders thought such behavior was unbelievable and, if true, it was crazy!

Our view was and still is: *'Their belief is good for them, and our belief is good for us.'* The sky is the roof and Earth is the floor of our church.

As youngsters, we didn't realize that white people believed we were cantankerous, slow-witted savages. Why would we? As young adults, we soon learned about outside hatred and killing. Meskwakis were fighting other tribes long before the arrival of the white people. Then, large areas of unoccupied land were available. If a tribe was more powerful, a weaker tribe could move rather than fight and sacrifice its people. The Chippewa, Huron, and other tribes helped push us from the northern reaches of the St. Lawrence River to the Mississippi River. The unbelievable numbers of aggressive, land grabbing white people and their superior weapons and diseases changed our world.

White people had the knowledge and ability to make and use muskets, tools, and materials that we couldn't duplicate. Also, they could write and read their words. In ways, we thought they were ignorant savages. Certainly, they had the might and will to kill us when it served their purpose to take our land or resources.

Uncle Leno once mused aloud, "Perhaps, just perhaps, the Frenchman's greatest invention was a merciful God who forgave followers all their earthly misdeeds and welcomed them to His Happy Hunting Grounds. All they had to do was confess their sins to ordained Jesuit Priests. I'll believe the French are as special as they think they are when they modify a Mother Earth reality, like flapping their arms and flying."

Many white people thought killing a Native American wasn't a sin, and we were just wild animals in their way. With all their knowledge and achievements, white people knew little about the best use of the land, water, and creatures provided by Wisaka, countless winters before they arrived.

Can you think of anything sillier than fencing land and growing grass and corn on land to feed hogs and cows for meat? When they could hunt awhile and kill delicious meat as needed. Mother Earth cared for Native American needs without strangling her land with fences. Early, our youngsters were taught how to use Nature's bounty. Many white people were slow to learn these skills or had little interest in learning.

White people's greatest talents were taking control of land, rivers, animals, or whatever they wanted. To this end, cheating and lying were justified. In addition, they tried to change our culture and killed us when it served their needs. To a Meskwaki, those actions are a much better description of ***savages***.

In our Kickapoo River village, we were busy playing, learning, working, farming, hunting, helping each other, and celebrating blessings. As children, we rarely knew hunger and felt secure from outside dangers. At a young age, we were taught to be independent and seldom punished for minor misbehavior. Of course, we had our share of challenges and problems, such as disagreements amongst ourselves, too cold, too hot, floods, mosquitos, accidents, and etc.

By the time of Vision Quests and recognition as adults, we learned our tribe often battled other tribes over rights to use land for hunting and farming. This led to war and killing. Wisaka molded many Meskwakis into great warriors to defend our lives, property, and honor.

Thanks to the greedy French and their gullible, easy-to-bribe Algonquian allies, our happy little village was caught up in the turmoil. Later, it was deserted and burned.[3]

---

[3] Appendix A is a timeline of the Meskwaki Tribe's key events (filled with conflicts and killings) before and during Tyr's lifetime.

My Family

In addition to Wisaka, my family and others helped mold this *dab of red clay* named Tyr.

Family living in our lodge included **Achak**, my father; **Anna**, my mother; **Mingan**, my older brother; **Alawa**, my older sister; **Nodin**, Achak's father; **Nadi**, Achak's sister; **Chogan** her husband; **Leno**, Anna's brother; **Wapun**, Anna's adopted sister; **Etchemin,** Wapun's husband. Counting Tyr, eleven lived in the lodge.

Achak was our civil chief. Earlier, he was a war chief for the largest Meskwaki village located near Big Lake Butte Des Morts about 150 miles east and north of our location. Achak discovered the Kickapoo River area when leading a hunting party.

Achak and Anna were tired of endless conflict with the French and allied tribes. They decided moving farther west would be less dangerous for their young family to be. Anna was pregnant with Mingan. On-again, off-again fights with the Sioux made the western side of the great Mississippi River unsafe. There were serious truce talks ongoing between the Sioux and Meskwaki. The Kickapoo (a brother tribe) had a village where the Kickapoo River joined the Wisconsin River. And, not too far north of the confluence of the Wisconsin and Mississippi rivers was a small Meskwaki village at Prairie du Chien.

The beautiful, bountiful Kickapoo River area was their choice. Anna believed they had found the land's happiest hunting ground. She was a loving and caring person with strong convictions. One of her favorite expressions was, *'Just do what's right!'*

As the village grew, each new family learned Achak was an excellent civil chief. By Meskwaki tradition, the civil chief of a Meskwaki village should be a member of the Bear Clan.

When our village was formed there were no Bear Clan members. As a result, Achak, a Fox Clan member, became Civil Chief Achak.

Aunt Nadi and Aunt Wapun were like extra mothers in our lodge. Anna, Nadi, and Wapun were helpful, friendly and seldom had a break from their hard work and busy lives.

Grandfather Nodin was above routine affairs, although he was in charge of growing tobacco. He was old, and so far in good health, with plenty of knowledge and experiences to share. If he couldn't snap you out of a feeling-low spell, you were really low or sick.

One of my favorite people was Uncle Etchemin. He taught me how to choose the best sap-producing trees and each step in the maple syrup-making process. I was his *'Sap Buddy.'* His wife, Aunt Wapun, a Chippewa by birth, was captured as a young girl by a Meskwaki war party from Uncle Etchemin's village. She was adopted and still later married Uncle Etchemin. Adopting those captured in war was common practice among tribes.

Aunt Wapun was a village favorite. Like Uncle Etchemin, she was a maple syrup expert. She and Uncle Etchemin were joyful people. Despite early hardships and heartbreak, she was full of love and always ready to help family, friends, or anyone she could assist.

Uncle Chogan, like Achak and Uncle Leno, was a proven warrior. Uncle Chogan was a vital member of the village. He was an expert Flintknapper (maker of flint tools, arrow or spear points, and fire strikers). Also, he had a serious problem—a great desire for French grape brandy, which turned him into a sloppy drunk when he could get it. Aunt Nadi constantly helped fight his problem. The rest of the family provided aid and support. No brandy was allowed in our lodge. Achak and the village council didn't ban brandy from the village. It was a lodge-by-lodge decision and there were others who drank brandy. Not often yet too often, Uncle Chogan's demon, turned him into a drunken fool.

A mother's brother in our village was responsible for guiding and teaching a nephew. I was beyond lucky because Uncle Leno was my teacher and frequent companion.

When younger, Uncle Leno canoed the network of rivers and great lakes from the eastern seashore, also down and up the Mississippi River. Earning honors as a fierce warrior, he was wounded several times. The last wound permanently crippled his left leg, preventing him from participating in war or hunting parties. He could still go where he wanted, although he had to half-drag his injured leg. With the help of his cane, he dragged that leg more miles than some of the healthy men walked or ran.

Uncle Leno often summarized talks by pronouncing, *"That's Life! It's crammed with wonder, happiness, sadness, and surprises."* Uncle Leno advised me many times, "Hush Tyr, talking closes your ears, so you can't learn." Sometimes he abbreviated his advice to "SHUT UP!" As already noted, Uncle Leno was a wise man.

I was six winters younger than Mingan, whose goal was to be a war chief. From the age of 12 winters, he was busy learning war tactics and the best way to defend against enemies and win battles. If asked for help, Mingan would lend me a hand, but was too involved with his interests to spend much time with his younger brother.

Sister Alawa was a constant and loyal companion as well as another supervisor until I was about 10 winters. Then I began spending more time with Keme, Chaska, and other friends. Alawa married and her new husband moved into our lodge, just before I left on a Mississippi River adventure.

Our lodge was an excellent place to sleep, eat, work, play games, and talk with family and friends, especially at night, during heavy rainfall or in the winter when surrounded by shivering cold, sleet, or snow. The smell of food on the fires and scented herbs helped overpower bad odors. During the day and when the weather cooperated, we spent all the time we could outside to escape close quarters and wood smoke.

The lodge was about 18 feet wide, 15 feet high, and 40 feet long. There were two fire pits and doors at each end, with smoke holes above each fire pit. Covers for these holes could be slid in place with long poles. A center aisle with platforms on both sides provided space for sitting, sleeping, and storage. Dried food hung from overhead frames and additional food was stored in a large hole dug near the west end of the lodge, and covered by reinforced mats. Other items, like snowshoes, were lashed to the frame.

We had a large council lodge, a communal storage lodge, a small tobacco storage lodge, a lodge where females stayed during their menstrual periods, and a sweat lodge. When I departed on a Mississippi River adventure, we had 30 lodges. Most of the Meskwakis from Prairie du Chien had relocated to our village, and the Kickapoo Tribe members located near the confluence of the Kickapoo and Wisconsin Rivers had moved south.

Best Friends—Keme and Chaska

Keme's presence is one of my earliest memories. He was a winter older and we often played together, fought with each other, and constantly competed. I competed while Keme easily won contests. He was the fastest, tallest, and strongest. He was so strong that Chaska claimed he had muscles in his hair that sometimes interfered with his brain. By the time Keme was sixteen winters, except for raw strength and weapon competitions, no villager could beat him in physical games or contests. He did fear heights, while I was the crazy kid who would be the first to jump or dive from the highest bluffs.

Chaska's family moved to our village when I was about 10 winters, and he was a winter younger. His father was a Meskwaki and his mother a Santee Dakota Sioux with some Sauk blood. He also had an older sister with a Sauk husband. Chaska was a little shorter than most village males about our age. When he first arrived, a village bully started picking on him. After witnessing it several times, I finally *did the right thing*. Interceding, I knocked the bully on his ass and luckily for me, Chaska became a lifelong friend.

Village divers soon learned Chaska had no fear of heights, and he had springs in his legs and gracefully soared from the highest places. He took over my role as first off the highest bluffs.

Keme's greatest expertise was tracking man or beast. It was a gift from Wisaka. When Keme stepped into the woods to track or hunt, his countenance changed as he absorbed the sights, sounds, and odors of the woods, animals, birds, and insects. He rubbed different colored stains and scents into his breechcloth, leggings, and moccasins to match the season, trying to become one with the forest. His favorite sport was laying hands on animals and birds. We called it counting coups.

Chaska and I have seen Keme touch a buffalo, a young grizzly bear, elk, deer, beaver, turkeys, and other smaller animals and birds.

When Keme, Chaska, and I were together, I did most of the talking. Keme did the difficult tasks, trusting Chaska and me for the simple work. Chaska made clear the best approach to whatever adventure, game, or task was at hand. Although the youngest, Chaska was the best at sign language and conversing in Meskwaki, Sioux, and French. Our Meskwaki language was soft and musical compared to the more guttural Sioux tongue, and it was fun listening to Chaska switch words back and forth between languages. He was an expert drummer and danced with special energy and rhythm. Chaska was brighter and had more talent than either Keme or your talker, perhaps more than the two of us together.

There were two village kinship groups—black and white. A father's firstborn would be placed in the group opposite from his group, then each younger child would alternate groups. My father, Achak, was in the white group; thus my brother, Mingan, was in the black, my sister, Alawa, was white, and I was black. The selections weren't based on clan or other factors. Instead, it was an easy way to quickly separate the village into two social groups for games, celebrations, and other village activities.

Keme and Chaska were in the white kinship group, so I competed against them in village competitions. Also, we were separated during celebrations or social activities when villagers were divided into two groups.

I was fortunate to have two loyal, talented, and outstanding friends—Keme and Chaska. The three of us later shared a Mississippi River adventure.

Atlatls

An atlatl contest, won by me, was associated with a large trade meeting held at Prairie du Chien, located a few miles north of the Mississippi and Wisconsin River confluence. Members of more than 10 tribes and 50 villages attended. Because of common welfare, at this trade meeting, a temporary truce agreement was established between otherwise unfriendly tribes and villages. More than 12 French traders and helpers were present.

Earlier, there was a small Meskwaki Village at this site. The chief's name was Alim. Nicolas Perrot (a French trader) built a trading post here. Alim means a dog in Meskwaki and Chien in French. Perrot named it Prairie du Chien—French for 'Dog's Prairie.' After a few summers of trading and lots of walking by Perrot, he traded muskets to our people, and we began calling him 'Iron Legs.'

Meskwakis didn't trust, or like most of the short, bearded, stinking, and scheming Frenchmen. Hating them came later, as we fought on-again and off-again wars with the French and their easily bribed Algonquian allies.

This trade meeting was held in the early spring after my eleventh winter. Nine other contestants, all much older than your talker, participated in the atlatl competitions. How could a boy win against these men? Two answers: Uncle Leno and many, many hours of determined practice!

Atlatls are ancient spear launchers now rarely used. Some villages had elders like Uncle Leno, who recognized atlatls were better than bows and arrows for some big game hunting.

In the hands of an expert, atlatls are more accurate at short distances and have more killing power than arrows. Atlatls are less effective in heavily wooded areas and slower to reload. Also, it's more challenging to become an atlatl expert than learning to accurately release arrows from a bow. For killing, we knew *good* muskets were better than all our silent weapons.

Before my seventh winter, Uncle Leno gave me a scaled-down atlatl. My enthusiasm for launching spears into a target earned high praise from Uncle Leno. This praise and sling-the-spears fun motivated many hours of practice, practice, and practice.

Soon I was making my own atlatls and spears. These are simple tasks; however when one tries to be the best, then simple becomes complex. The quality of atlatls and spears is as important for precise accuracy as one's slinging skill. Achieving the best took a lot of work, concentration, patience, and help from Uncle Leno and Uncle Chogan.

Uncle Leno helped set up an area to store the materials and tools needed to make precision atlatls and spears. Here I worked and practiced slinging skills. We needed fire for many tasks like keeping fingers warm, pine resins soft for gluing, and heat to help straighten spears. Uncle Chogan donated a flint striker that started a lot of fires. Uncle Leno spent part of his time making sure I knew what and how to safely do the work and convinced Anna and Achak it was safe for me to work alone. After some demonstrations, they agreed it was OK.

Uncle Chogan was the village arrow-spear head expert. He knew where to find used ones. Many were found around old Indian Mounds near our village and along the lowlands next to rivers and creeks. If needed, he could reshape those found or chip new ones. He explained why obsidian and flint are the best arrow and spear point materials. For accuracy, obsidian is the best. Its sharper, smoother edges, and surfaces improve accuracy and distance when formed into a point. Most obsidian comes from mountains hundreds of miles west of the Mississippi River. The good news was it could be obtained by trading, and Uncle Chogan had plenty that he shared with me. Most villagers called Uncle Chogan, 'Flintknapper.'

I swapped and tested hundreds of different atlatl and spear combinations. It became an obsession. Most of my spare moments were spent trying to improve atlatls, spears, and slinging skills. Keme thought so much time with atlatls was time wasted. Chaska shared my enthusiasm and spent a lot of time working with me, learning how to make atlatls and sling spears. During these work sessions, he taught me essential stuff, like how to say 'kiss my ass' in French and Sioux.

Uncle Leno declared that I won the Prairie du Chien accuracy contest because of skill and focus, and I won the distance contest because of divine help. A wind manitou grabbed my spear and helped it fly about 80 feet farther than it should have.

The real craziness happened after the contests. A few competitors asked to try slinging spears with my atlatl. They were pleased with the results and wanted to trade for my atlatl and spears. Uncle Leno was watching and listening and asked one of the fellows, a minor Santee Dakota Sioux chief, how much he was willing to offer. The chief, with dancing words, finally offered two beaver skins for the atlatl and two for three spears.

Uncle Leno became the negotiator and others, including Achak, became interested in the bartering. My negotiator countered, "Tyr can kill and dress 12 beavers in the time it takes to make an atlatl or three spears having the quality of these. And, remember what the boy did with them."

Confirming Uncle Leno's remark, one of the bystanders, a bearded, heavyset French trader, spoke out, "Yeah, that young blue-eyed bastard really can throw those spears." I didn't understand his words. Achak could both understand and speak a lot of French. In a heartbeat, he was in front of the Frenchman, telling him he was my father and demanding an apology for the remark. The Frenchman pulled his knife! I had never seen

Achak completely lose his temper or jump into action. Neither had the Frenchman.

Before he could make a move, the Frenchman was on the ground, with Achak on top of him, pressing the knife against his throat. Cooler heads, including Uncle Leno and a friend of the Frenchman, helped prevail. Before he had his throat cut, the Frenchman shouted, "I apologize, I apologize, Jesus Christ, I apologize! I didn't mean anything bad, but the blue eyes had to come from someone else." With our honor satisfied, Achak placed the knife in the Frenchman's sheath, bounced off him, and helped him up like nothing had happened. Since I couldn't understand the French words; Uncle Leno later explained what happened. He could converse in Meskwaki, Sioux, and French.

After the confrontation, it took a while for my nerves to settle. We eventually accepted and collected offers of six made beaver (MB) skins[4] for an atlatl and six MB skins for three spears. Having brought a backup atlatl and several more spears, we made two trades and collected 24 MB skins. For the same price, two other buyers placed orders. Those interested in improving atlatl skills were willing to part with some of their wealth to improve their equipment.

A list of items we could receive for one MB skin were: A gallon of brandy, a yard of duffel cloth, two yards of cotton, two yards of flannel, one blanket, two shirts, one pair of breeches, one pair of shoes, 12 dozen buttons, 3/4 lb. of colored beads, two pairs of looking glasses, two pounds of sugar, one pound of salt, five pecks of Indian corn, four pecks of Indian meal, two pints of gunpowder, one pint of shot, six knives, two axes or hatchets, two hoes, 20 flints, 20 fish hooks, one bear

---

[4] MB (Made Beaver) furs meant the beavers had been killed with heavy coats during the winter, they met a minimum size and the furs properly skinned and processed. Furs not meeting the MB standards could be bartered, but weren't as valuable.

skin, one otter skin, two fox skins, two woodchuck skins, eight mink skins, four raccoon skins, or five pounds of feathers.

It took six MB skins to purchase a pistol and 12 skins for a musket and these were trader prices. For us, it was like stealing, because many items were impossible for us to duplicate.

As the crow flies, Prairie du Chien was about 30 miles from our village and 50 miles by canoe. Ten of us paddled five canoes to the event. Unfortunately, Keme had to stay home because of an injured ankle. We brought 18 beaver pelts, other trading goods, and a long list of items the village needed. Our atlatl windfall was a gift from Wisaka. We returned home with some of the trading goods still in the canoes. In addition, we came back with pots, blankets, beads, knives, hatchets, hoes, cotton, and flannel cloth, one musket, two pistols, shot, gunpowder, flints, fish hooks, and 10 birch bark containers filled with parched rice.

Trading was still busy when our group of canoes left Prairie du Chien. Leaving early was common practice.

Before we left, a young Menominee girl was reported missing by her frantic family, who thought foul play was involved. The word quickly spread and reports claimed that earlier two other girls had been found in the area strangled and with their left-breast nipples sliced off. Since we would be paddling downstream, the distraught father asked Achak to watch for signs of his daughter.

Achak agreed and promised to return if he found anything of interest. He and Uncle Etchemin were a team, and would be last in our five-canoe group. Uncle Leno and I came together and were second in the group. We were to stay within visible range of the canoe in front. Alternate canoes would focus on the left and right banks. If the canoes in front didn't see anything, they would continue to our village. Uncle Leno and I nor anyone in front of us failed to notice anything suspicious.

We lost sight of the canoe behind us. This was curious. Following orders, we continued homeward.

The canoe behind us found the young Menominee girl, someone had strangled and cut off her left nipple. Achak and Etchemin unloaded enough trade goods to the other canoes, wrapped the young victim in a blanket, and paddled back to Prairie du Chien. The girl's grieving father told Achak that he found a distinct mocassin print on the bank where someone had dragged her to the water. They were going to sketch the imprint and show it to nearby villages.

When he returned home, Achak proclaimed that we outsmarted the traders and announced a special celebration. He shared the serial killer information and warned our young females and families to be extremely vigilant.

It was no longer a rumor. There was a crazy murderer in our midst. We all made efforts to collect evidence and find the killer. Warnings were sent to villages near Prairie du Chien. Young girls and women were cautioned to be watchful and not leave their villages alone.

No further killings were reported for two winters and no additional clues found. So the search for the killer fizzled. Then he or a copycat killed another girl on the other side of the Mississippi River. Once again fear reigned, but no other killings were reported and the killer wasn't found.

I continued to build and sell atlatls until the Mississippi River adventure. Chaska became a full-time helper and an excellent spear slinger. The atlatl work became drudgery, so Chaska's help and ideas were welcomed relief. During breaks, he continued to share his boundless knowledge, including how to pronounce a few more choice French and Sioux words I couldn't repeat in front of Anna or my aunts.

Aunt Meda

Late summer after my Atlatl competition, the village affairs seemed normal, and I was still being treated like a young boy. Now as an old man, I can add hindsight to early memories. Aunt Meda, whom I met once for less than two days, was the most impressive person I've ever known!

One fire-circle evening, Anna informed us, "My older sister, a prophetess, healer, and magician, is coming to our village. On her last visit 12 winters ago, your Aunt Meda came here with her husband, a Dutch trapper. They left their two boys with family in New York, a great village near the eastern sea. As children, Meda and I shared almost everything. She will be here in a few days, and I can't wait to see her."

Excitement bubbled in the village, especially in our lodge, and everyone seemed to be cleaning and preparing for a momentous occasion. Meda's emissary, a tall Sauk named Many Feathers, arrived two days later. He reported that Meda would be here before midday tomorrow and her presence would be announced by two loud musket blasts, which I believed was strange.

Late the following morning, more than 120 village residents and about 12 visitors were milling around in the commons area between our lodges and the river.

WHAM! WHAM! Our eyes were drawn down the river, where a large canoe slowly advanced toward us. We could make out two paddlers, front and back, with a person balanced on an elevated seat in the center. With such a large, high center of gravity, it appeared the canoe could easily tip over. Yet, they paddled upstream with apparent ease, and Many Feathers met them at the river's edge. He helped land the canoe. Then with a flourish, he helped Meda ashore. She faced us and raised both arms high over her head, waving them back and forth with open palms. Next she showered the crowd with thrown kisses.

Gawking eyes watched as she came up the inclined pathway. The two paddlers lifted her seat, which was a large box, and trudged along behind. Many Feathers carried the longest musket we had ever seen. The men walked with heads bobbing up and down while an ever-erect Meda, smoothly glided up the path.

Meda was a not-fat big woman and almost six feet tall. Without her breasts, I would have guessed she was a man. As she came nearer, it was clear she had the soft, pretty face of a woman and resembled Anna. She wore a striking red cape trimmed along the sides and bottom with thin, soft white fur, and along the top with black material. The garment was covered with intricate patterns of white beads sewn to look like birds, perhaps hawks. A handsome, dyed black, beaver fur cap was attached and hanging at the top back of her cape.

She pulled the cape around her, so her arms were hidden. Her smiling eyes were searching for Anna, who quickly stepped forward. Aunt Meda opened her cape, and they fell into each other's arms. Closing the cape and clutching Anna, Aunt Meda openly wept and kept repeating, "My beautiful precious little sister." Finally, she opened the cape and allowed Anna, with streaming tears, to escape. Still holding hands, Anna presented Aunt Meda to Achak, and the three of them had a quiet, brief conversation. Then Achak introduced Meda and asked all to face the common's area with backs to the river so we could better view the proceedings and hear her words.

Meda confidently stepped to the front of the crowd. She declared in a loud, lyrical voice, **"YOU ARE SPECIAL!"** Pausing to let her words sink in, she continued, "What a wonderful day! Can't you hear the spirits singing? Today, oak sap tastes like honey, and the beavers are grinning. Even the fish are smiling. What a joy it is to be here with family and friends. You've already met Many Feathers. Let me introduce my son, Balli, and his friend Ahanu."

Already, individuals in the crowd were happy. In a few moments, Meda had made new friends, and we were interested in what she would say and do.

Meda continued, "We will have fun and show you things you've not seen. Some will say you witnessed magic. We call it training, misdirection, and using the right equipment. You'll be the judge."

She flipped both hands up, and out flew a sparrow from each hand. Quickly, she mingled with the crowd, shaking hands with young and old, pulling trinkets and beads out of youngsters' ears and noses and leaving them as treasures. Each of the excited children had wide-open eyes beaming the same question: *How did she do that?*

While she was working the crowd, Balli and Ahanu moved the canoe-seat box to front and center. Meda then took a position behind the box and lifted out a bag. She told Balli, "Please take my medicine bag and put it in a cool place in the lodge." Reaching back into the box, she pulled out a knife and two necklaces she had pilfered while in the crowd. No one could believe she removed their adornments in broad daylight without their knowledge. Going back into the crowd, she handed each to the correct owner. Then she stopped near me and asked, "Did everyone have their belongings returned?" I felt for my knife. It had disappeared, so I held up my hand and reported it gone. She seemed surprised. Then pointing to an oak tree, she had not been near, she said, "Blue Eyes, your knife is behind that tree." Unbelievably, it was there. Earlier, she hadn't stopped, only slightly bumped me as she passed by.

Meda then advised, "Mothers with small children need to move to the far left, as Many Feathers is going to prove his expertise with the long musket. He will do it on the far right, trying not to scare our youngsters. The rest of us need to leave space on the right so he can safely shoot toward the river."

Many Feathers cradled a long musket in his arms and pompously strode about, stoking our curiosity, and raising a bit of ill will with his overbearing demeanor. Our suspicions quickly turned to *laughter* when he tripped over his feet and sprawled to the ground. He jumped up, smiled, and nimbly moved to the firing position while showing and telling us, "This specially made Dutch double-barreled flintlock musket is one of the best muskets ever made. I can fire both rounds in less than 15 seconds."

Meda, who had a wood duck in her hand, shouted, "Let's see you hit this duck!" She flung it in the air toward him. While at close range and clear of the crowd, the duck was flapping its wings. Many Feathers fired. WHAM! He not only missed, but the recoil knocked him to the ground, and the frightened duck accelerated toward the river. The look of disbelief on the shooter's face was hilarious, and the crowd laughed at him again.

Many Feathers, while on his butt, calmly switched barrels and pulled the trigger. WHAM! This time the distant duck turned into a shower of feathers. We realized a well-staged act and an excellent marksman had tricked us. Many Feathers wasn't pompous or awkward, and he just wanted us to enjoy the shooting exhibition.

About this time, Balli and Ahanu commenced whooping and performing a wild jumping dance while juggling balls. Eventually, eight of them were in the air at the same time. Meda set the pace with equally wild and entertaining drum beating. Before their act became tiring, Meda moved to the big box, and pulled out a piece of leather which she wrapped, and secured around her right wrist and lower arm. Next, Meda lifted a smaller box, housing a large, hooded hawk. She placed the hawk on her leather armband and then removed the hood. It perched there, blinking its eyes, and adjusting to the new surroundings.

"Say hello to my huntress friend, Sally," Meda invited, then continued, "She is an eight winters, red-tailed hawk trained to bring me birds. Girls sometimes have to hunt too." With another flourish, Meda reached with her empty left hand and appeared to grab a sparrow out of the air, which she pitched upward; it immediately streaked toward the river. Meda unleashed Sally, who caught the sparrow then swooping low over our heads Sally returned to her arm perch with the sparrow in her beak and was rewarded with a treat. After this, she repeated the maneuver several times so we could all get a good look at Sally, the huntress, flying close over the children's heads. Sally was hooded and returned to her box.

With the crowd buzzing, Meda performed a few more magic tricks before turning to Balli and asking him to retrieve her medicine bag. She needed to visit our sick people. Plucking another sparrow from thin air with her left hand and then a small hawk with her right hand, Meda said, "Let's see if Many Feathers is an excellent marksman or lucky." Then she pitched both birds above her head. Many Feathers, standing with his back to Meda, raised the musket, and WHAM he obliterated the first bird, a sparrow, before it made the river. Switching barrels, it took a few seconds as the hawk was gaining altitude and distance. WHAM! The hawk seemed to jump a little, then turned toward us and returned to Aunt Meda's open hands. Meda laughingly explained, "Many Feathers is a great marksman, especially when he shoots toward one of my favorite birds."

She pointed at me, and asked, "Blue Eyes will you go see what happened to Balli?" Entering the cluttered lodge, I looked into all possible hiding places, and Balli wasn't there. So, I reported him missing. She replied, "You never know what he will do." Peering down the river with a hand above her eyes, she asked, "Could he be coming up the river?" We all knew that would be impossible. Balli had just entered the lodge and could not be paddling up the river. The paddler, in a great hurry beached the canoe, and hustled up the path toward us. Balli was carrying the medicine bag. As he apologized to Meda for taking so long, the rest of us were shocked. *This had to be magic.*

A smiling Meda raised her hand and explained, "We wanted to show you there are plausible explanations for many events appearing to be magic." Then she yelled, "Balli!" And he appeared from behind the lodge with the medicine bag in hand. Standing side-by-side, you couldn't tell Balli from the stranger. Putting her arm around the stranger, Meda said that, I want you to meet Belli—my second son and twin of Balli. He's been hiding down the river, waiting for the second series of two quick blasts from Many Feathers. This was the signal for Belli to bring the medicine bag. The bag is a duplicate without the medicine.

"We have tried to show that with the right setting, timing, and trained actors, events that seem like magic can be created. Nature's version of magic is much greater than ours. If you haven't been fooled by reflections of light, sounds bouncing off objects, or the actual size of something first seen from a distance, then you are a youngster, or you are sleepwalking through life."

Meda and helpers held us spellbound and left most of us with puzzled faces.

Next, Meda, along with our medicine man and his helper, Kanti, visited the sick people in our village.

After gorging at the days feast, people rested in their lodges, on the riverbank, or went about their business. Anna and Aunt Meda went to our lodge. I was close behind, because I wanted to know how she knew where my knife was. She was seated, so I crouched at her feet and asked my question. Aunt Meda motioned to sit, patted my head, and answered, "Blue Eyes it's easy to trick you. Once a person is skilled and has quick hands, and fingers, it's simple to borrow a knife. You do it by distracting and touching the person with one hand or your body while borrowing with the other hand." Then she handed back my knife that she borrowed a second time.

With an old, small, and worn-smooth Dutch guilder coin, she showed how nimble her fingers were. By motion of fingers only, she could move the coin between her thumb and fingers with either hand. Next, she returned my knife for the third time. I was caught watching her right-hand fingers nimbly bounce a coin along the top of her fingers, while she again 'borrowed' my knife with her left hand.

Finally, she answered my question: In a magic act the audience can't keep up with each movement of the actors on a stage. Your common's area was our stage; We have a trick we call bait and double-switch. I brought your knife to the big box with the other borrowed items; When Balli came to pick up my medicine bag, he also picked up your knife and hid it in his sleeve; I was baiting the crowd by returning the other borrowed items; Balli brushed and passed your knife to Many Feathers. And I watched him drop the knife behind the Oak tree. We have practiced and performed the trick many times so it was easy.

It is easy to fool people, if you are trained and set up the right circumstances. After trying to work Aunt Meda's coin between my fingers, I realized the 'if' factor could be huge. I tried to return her coin. She said, "You keep it and practice. Your blue eyes are reminders of my precious husband and how helpful and peace-loving some white people are, especially the Dutch."

Saving the coin, I later included it in my medicine pouch. I practiced moving it between my fingers many times, and slow progress made me spend my time at more pressing matters.

Before Aunt Meda's appointment to speak with our village council, she invited me to sling a few spears. I jumped at the opportunity to show her my expertise at something. The atlatl practice site was close at hand. A small group, including Uncle Leno, joined us at the unplanned target practice. Aunt

Meda said that she and her little brother (Uncle Leno) were good slingers. We were taught by our father, who was an excellent slinger.

I asked if she would like to sling some practice spears and was surprised when she smiled at Uncle Leno, and answered, “Thanks, I am ready to go. You are right-handed. So am I.” Handing her my atlatl and a spear, she didn’t make excuses about lack of practice or being rusty. She only remarked, “Goodness, both the atlatl and spears are lighter than I remember. I will sling three spears, then you sling three, and we will see who gets closest to the target’s center.” Next, she flexed her right arm a few times. Her stance and flipping motion, made it obvious she was no amateur. Her first spear found the higher right side of the target. The second was about six inches low and a few inches right of the target’s marked center, and her final throw was the exact height and about three inches left of the center. I told her, “I am glad you didn’t have more practice tosses.”

She had no idea how often I had aimed spears at this target. The target was 35 feet away, and I knew exactly where to stand for different conditions and promptly put a spear about halfway between her best effort and the target’s center and the second less than an inch right. Not bragging, but I planted the third one dead center. The small crowd responded with energetic clapping. Aunt Meda hugged this atlatl boy and declared, “Father would be so proud of your atlatl skill, just like your Uncle Leno and Aunt Meda.” I was bursting with pride as we returned to the lodge. So was Uncle Leno.

Immediately I found Achak and asked permission to hear Aunt Meda’s talk. He answered, “You can’t take a seat. Since she’s your aunt, if you can find a corner, then squeeze into it.” I went directly to the council lodge, staked out a corner, squeezed in, and remained there throughout her talk.

Meda entered like a queen with her red cape, bearing, and gliding motion. This was the essence of her talk to a hanging-on-each-word council:

I'm happy to touch hearts with you. With my husband, Rikki, I spent the last 20 winters, more than half-of-my life, in New York, a large town near the great sea's eastern shore. I learned to speak the Dutch language and read their books and papers. I will tell you truths seen and heard from my eyes and ears.

Two winters ago, Rikki and a good friend went hunting north of Lake Ontario. Neither returned. They disappeared. After much searching, we found nothing to explain their disappearance. They were just gone. It could have been an accident. However, as you know, we live in a dangerous world.

For many winters, I watched large ships empty their cargos of people and trade goods. Then, the ships were loaded with our furs, corn, fish, wood, and maple syrup. It slows at times but doesn't stop. This is the same for docks along the eastern and southern seas. Most people coming to our land are English or their European neighbors.

Most French and Spanish immigrants are interested in what they can take away, not settling, although many stay. The Dutch hardly count, and they are so small in number, and the English now control the land the Dutch once claimed. The English want to buy our land with baubles, push us off or kill us so they can own and divide it like the land they left.

Last summer, I decided to return to my Sauk homeland. We came by way of Detroit, where the French built Fort Pontchartrain and have surrounded it with easy-to-bribe tribes, including Ottawa, Huron, Illinois, and Chippewa. Your people once controlled this area, and I understand some of your leaders are considering moving a village there. I would only say, Don't underestimate French treachery!

With their muskets and scheming intrigue, many white people are trying to change our culture, take our land, carry off our valuable goods, herd us like animals, treat us like slaves, or kill us when it serves their purposes;

Our best hope is to band together and use their muskets to force them back to Europe or kill them. Otherwise, we will lose our freedom and land. White people may already outnumber us, and the chance of our diverse tribes banding together to fight is close to zero. Many, including our Algonquian cousins, believe the French, English, or Spanish people are more trustworthy than their tribal cousins;

Most tribes west of the Mississippi River have no idea how serious the threat is to their way of life. A few southern tribes are trying to hold off the Spanish. However, the western tribes are too busy defending hunting grounds and shooting arrows at each other to join a battle against the white people;

Only Kehci Manitou can know how this will end. Without divine intervention, our people will suffer terrible tribulations; Then, Meda opened the meeting for questions and discussion.

Achak pointed his finger at me, then at the exit. I knew he was sorry I had heard Aunt Meda's message.

Later that night, our lodge fires were flickering and all seemed asleep except Anna and Aunt Meda. They moved to my end of the lodge, thinking I was sleeping. Anna kept asking Aunt Meda about her New York experiences. My eyes were closed, but my ears were on high alert:

Anna, you were too young to remember when Rikki first came to our village, trading for fur. Like other trappers, he didn't stay long. He did keep returning and became good friends with our father. They traded and killed game together. Rikki was welcome in our lodge. He learned to speak our language and entertained us with quick hands and tricks;

After I was sixteen winters and unmarried, his eyes and manners suggested a romantic interest, although he said nothing until he returned the next winter and asked for my hand in marriage. By then, you were old enough to remember him. Village men had little interest in me. I was too tall, not very pretty, and talked too much. Rikki wasn't pushy, but made it clear he thought I was special. I liked and admired him, but wasn't ready to marry anyone. When he returned the next winter and said, 'You are still special.' I agreed to the marriage. I learned he used the expression: ***'You are Special'*** like a calling card. In his memory, now I often use it. Rikki made clear I would be living with him in New York. With him, I felt safe, secure, and loved. Still, swapping locations and families was scary;

At first, I desperately missed my family and way of life. Happily, the good days were plentiful and filled with interesting activities. Rikki treated me like a treasure, and our love blossomed. His family, from the first day, accepted and helped my adjustment to the new life;

It was a busy life. Rikki's brother, Steffen is a doctor whom I later worked seven winters as his assistant. Steffen's daughter, Neske, was two winters older and became my mentor and loving friend. Neske taught me to read, write, and speak the Dutch language fluently, and so many other things I cannot count;

I soon found I was in a nest of magicians. Adults and children daily practiced magic tricks. They were members of *The Sorenson Family Magic Act*. With a few winters of practice, I too, became part of the act. That's how I became a skilled magician. We played to crowds from Boston to Baltimore. These are large towns north and south of New York;

One of my favorite activities was spending a day with Rikki, crossing the Hudson River by boat, and visiting New York. We mingled with the crowds, trying new foods, and watching thousands of other people. Lots of them watched us. A white man walking side by side with a Sauk female was rare. Sometimes we walked the wharves and watched swarms of people unloading from the big ships.

I dozed off. My next recall was Aunt Meda being fully dressed and preparing to return to her mother's and my grandmother's Sauk Village.

After Aunt Meda departed, I never saw her again or knew what happened to her or her team. Like her husband, Rikki, and others, they just mysteriously vanished. Her skills, presence, energy, friendliness, heart, achievements, and wisdom were an incredible combination. I hoped some of her, whatever it was, rubbed off on me.

Storm From Hell

My first hunting trip with a group of village hunters is a seared-into-my-head memory. Being 12 winters old, I was the youngest member of a 12-man hunting party. Also, my friend Keme was in the party. Our leader, Kailo, was an expert hunter, who each man in the hunting party respected. Since no one in the village could match my atlatl skills, I felt I earned the chance to hunt with elders.

It was late summer, and the days were long and hot. Thunderstorms were common and welcome for cooling and watering our crops. If protective shelter wasn't available, bad storms could be a serious problem.

Kailo decided our best chance for well-fed deer or elk was in a valley about half-a-day north and a half-a-day west of our village. We left before sunrise. Along with weapons, we brought hickory poles to help transport the game.

We were on a bluff overlooking the chosen valley a couple of hours before dark. There was a sizeable herd of white-tail deer and about 12 elk grazing on grass and sprouts. Kailo was disappointed because there were fewer animals here than on previous hunts. He believed this meant more hunters were in the area or some unknown natural event had occurred. He split us into two groups. Keme stayed with Kailo while I was assigned to the group led by Ullich.

Ullich's group worked their way to the north of the valley while Kailo's group circled to the south. We were to be in place before the morning sun and limit our kills to seven or eight animals, which meant some of us wouldn't get credit for a kill.

Ullich, a big wiry man, was about 30 winters old. He was an excellent marksman with the bow, a superior hunter, and a brave warrior. Also, he was an abrasive braggart who had little patience for others' shortcomings. He stopped the group and with a tone of disgust, declared, “Tyr, you walk like a pregnant squaw and make too much noise. Walk more on your toes and watch where you step. Put your feet down on solid ground, not branches and pay special attention when you step over logs!”

It was an uncomfortable night, worrying about making noise and bringing down an elk or deer. Before dawn, I nibbled on pemmican and forced thoughts away from cramping muscles and Anna’s hot corn cakes smeared with crushed blackberries. Now I was a hunter, not a pampered boy whose village work included picking berries and gathering wood.

Dawn didn’t break, rather it lingered while the sun and clouds teased us with a slow dance. Darkness finally diffused into a light orange glow along the eastern skyline. Then gradually, a hazy white uncovered the nearby bluffs and trees.

The herd was collecting. Animals came from the woods in small groups; soon, they were busy feeding on the lush valley grass, sprouts, and tender bushes.

Deer are fond of cedar sprouts, peeking out of the ground in uncountable numbers. Elk like to graze on grass and herbs and often feed with deer. This morning, feeding contentedly together, they lifted their heads, and sniffed the air, constantly on the lookout for predators like us. Deer are social animals. Females and young males travel together in herds, similar to buffalos. Each herd has an alpha doe who warns the others when danger is approaching by loudly snorting and stamping her front hoofs.

We moved closer and could hear soft grunts. Deer make three distinct sounds—snorts, bleats, and grunts. They only grunt when contented and comfortable.

The animals were calm while I was tight as a bowstring and needed to relax. Glancing at Ullich, he was concentrating on the animals and also appeared to be tighter than a bow string. This random thought eased my tension.

Kailo's group was to initiate the action and we were alerted by the commotion started on the valley's opposite end and animals heading our way. Taking a few steps, I was in launching position and picked my target—a young well-fed elk. A deer brushed past, so I sidestepped the deer and hurled a spear into the elk's side. It made one jump and took several stumbling steps. An arrow from Ullich dropped her in a convulsing heap. Then she was still.

In front of us was bedlam! Frightened deer and elk bolted away from their attackers while Hunters traded arrows and spears for food. The killing was over, almost before it began, with Ullich yelling, **"No More! No More!"**

We killed seven deer and two elk. Kailo and Ullich were pleased. Quickly the animals were gutted and pulled to the valley's eastern side. Most hunters worked at retrieving arrows and spears, lashing carcasses to carrying poles, and covering the meat with leaves to protect it from flies. Several others built a roaring fire and roasted two deer for an impromptu meal. We had to leave one gutted deer along with the guts. Mother Nature's cleanup crew would be here before we were a mile away.

Desert—back-slapping tales of our shared hunting prowess—was served with the meal. Keme and I knew our places and held our tongues. No one enjoyed the meat more than us. We shared in the kills and were recognized for our contributions.

There wasn't much time for feasting or funning. Shouldering heavy loads, we headed home. The world was good. Hunting was great. The chief's boy proved he could sling his atlatl spear under pressure.

Feeling good was short-lived. A *Storm from Hell* found us the next day. We slept on the trail and began the southward trek toward home early in the morning. My focus was using my toes and silent walking. Kailo's group of six, with the two elk and largest deer left first, and we followed, although soon we were about a half-mile behind Kailo's group. Before long, we were on the trail adjacent to the Kickapoo River. Most of the flatland along the river was to our right. Farther right, the mountain bluffs looked like giant warriors guarding the land and crooked river below.

Across the river, huge clouds filled the sky. A flash of jagged lightning and a clap of thunder alerted us to pending trouble. A nearby bluff housed a large cave and safety. Trotting as fast as we could toward the cave, clumps of ice began falling.

Dropping our loads, we raced to nearby trees. Soon the wind settled, and ice stopped falling. Retrieving the game, we began picking a way through the ice. Across the river, more clouds were less than a mile away. Ullich yelled, **"Look!"** Several rotating clouds were weaving and dancing. The clouds became one. It headed toward us. Ullich shouted, **"Run!"** Terrified, we again dropped the deer and ran toward the trees. Before reaching the larger trees, the wind roared, whipping us almost off the ground. I stumbled into a shallow ditch. Ullich screamed, "Stay under me and hold on!" Grabbing a sapling growing from the ditch bottom, I held on with both hands.

The noise was roaring madness, and the wind a howling devil! I could hear, smell, and feel it all. I couldn't see because instinct instantly closed my eyes. Ullich's body impacted mine like he had been hit with a big rock. Then he was gone! I thought, "Hold on, hold on!" My mind left. It came back. I was cold and flying. Flashing bolts of lightning opened my eyes. Ullich was above. He was impaled by a large tree limb, twisting inside clouds with other tree branches, and hail. 'A foolish dream,' I thought as a feeling of quiet serenity replaced complete panic and fear.

My next memory was standing in mud without knowing what had happened or where I was. Someone yelled, "Tyr! Tyr!" Reality started to return. The voice crossed a small stream and grabbed my bloody hand. An emerging mind knew the wind had taken Ullich to the upper world and spit me out like a putrid morsel. I felt no pain, no anything. On some level, *I felt everything.*

Kailo had a better view of the scene as his group gained the cave's safety, and was looking down at us when the storm hit. This was his report to the village council:

We were returning from a successful hunt. The 12 of us had split into two groups, I led the first and Ullich led the second. We were moving south along the trail near the Kickapoo. Lightning and thunder told us to seek shelter. Fortunately, a big cave about nine miles from the village was close at hand;

Storing our game inside the cave, we moved back to the cave's entrance. Ullich's group came into view, and it started raining ice. Ullich and hunters dropped their loads and hurried to the shelter of trees. The ice stopped falling. They retrieved their loads and resumed a fast pace toward us. It was a strange scene. Upside down animals appeared to be pulling and pushing skaters on the ice;

Blackened clouds that brought the ice circled us. Beyond the river, three giant whirlwind clouds bobbed, weaved, and danced up and down like crazy brandy drunks trying to get in step;

Then! Then the whirlwinds joined, becoming one—a *Storm from Hell*. It headed toward Ullich's group. They dropped their game and again ran toward the trees. The Storm cut down trees like tender grass being sawed off or pulled from the ground. It passed over the river, sucking it up like a sip of water. Frantically we cowered into the cave's interior, but couldn't hide from terrifying noises, whipping wind, and darkness from Hell;

The air was cold and thick with debris and mud. You couldn't see your hands. It sounded like the world outside our cave was being ground into pieces. Then the wind was gone. Its fury trailed off to the west with a sullen, decreasing moan. Thankfully, the insanity didn't last long;

We stumbled out of the cave and found a scene of unbelievable destruction. The *Storm from Hell* had cut a trail of death about a quarter-mile wide. Before its might, trees were broken or gone. The trees were not cut down like tender grass. Instead, they were ripped and torn apart. Perhaps part of the noise was trees screaming from a fate they couldn't escape. In a trance, we scrambled from the cave and down the bluff toward where we had seen Ullich;

Regaining my senses, I organized a search for our brothers. Keme found Machk wandering in the nearby woods. He was incoherent and had a few minor cuts and bruises. One of the deer carcasses was found hanging in a broken oak tree. I saw a figure stumbling around in the mud. Minutes earlier, this mud was covered by the Kickapoo River. I thought it was Tyr and called his name. There was no answer. Jumping rocks and wading in mud, I grabbed his bloody hand. As the river refilled, I washed off mud and blood. Abrasions covered his bare skin, and a little finger appeared broken. Dazed, with wobbly legs and a shaky voice, Tyr mumbled, 'Ullich is in the Upper World';

No sign of Ullich, Hasun, Little Bear, or Grey Wolf was found. They may never be found. A search party needs to make a broader search.

The search party found no trace of Ullich or Little Bear. The battered bodies of Hasun and Grey Wolf were found, close together, about a half mile in the storm's direction.

We had our village burial rituals, followed by burials and mock burials for those whose bodies were missing. Those buried had their feet pointing west, so their spirits would head toward the Happy Hunting Ground.

Within 30 days, much of the deepest mourning had subsided. Except for a few scars, Machk and I were physically in good shape. Experiencing how quickly happiness can give way to great sorrow, took away some joy from our lives.

Uncle Leno told me, “Tyr, Wisaka has a special plan for you. How else would you survive almost certain death after being sucked into the sky?” That was a possibility. A definite outcome was my lifelong fear of thunderstorms.

Fire Circles

Scattered about the village and close to the lodges were several fire pits. We used them to cook meals. Frequently, during late afternoons and early evenings, families or members of a clan would gather around a pit. They would build a fire, bring mats to sit on, and completely encircle the pit. Adults would point their feet at the fire. Then, take turns telling stories. Young people would squeeze in between the adults. Here we learned about manitous, magic, funny stuff, scary stuff, heroic acts of our warriors or others, activity reports, upcoming celebrations, gossip, plans, crops, and you name it.

These meetings were called ***fire circles*** and were an essential and fun part of our existence. Grandparents, parents, and elders told us many stories about the present and the past, including stories about our ancestors. The eldest person told the first story of each session. Young people at least 10 winters old were encouraged to participate, especially when not much else was happening.

One of the fire circle stories recited by Aunt Nadi, who taught many youngsters how to plant and successfully grow corn, follows:

Wisaka made corn, our most important crop. Each grain has its own manitou, and when they are removed from the cob and wasted, they are unhappy. When we eat corn, each grain's little manitou goes into our bodies, making us stronger. We can do more work or travel farther, after eating corn than other foods. Making each grain's manitou happy makes us feel satisfied and happy too;

Corn is easy to plant and grow. It tastes good and can be stored and used in many ways. So, when you are working with corn or eating boiled corn, corn on the cob, corn cakes, popped corn, or hominy, take a little time to thank Wisaka for such a wonderful gift.

§§§

Anna followed this story by telling us how Wisaka first provided corn to Meskwakis:

Two ancient ancestors killed a deer and were sitting by a fire roasting it when a beautiful woman dropped from the sky and sat beside them. They were amazed and guessed she smelled the meat and was hungry, so they gave her a piece of the roasted deer. After eating, she told them to wait one year then return to the spot where she was sitting, and they would find a reward for their generosity. Suddenly, like a mysterious bird, she ascended to the cloudy sky and disappeared;

Returning to their village, they reported this strange experience and were laughed at by the people. When the year was up, a few villagers accompanied the two storytellers to the spot where their reward was waiting;

Where her right hand touched, they found corn growing. Where her left hand touched, beans were growing, and where she sat, tobacco was growing.

One morning after corn stories, I was working on atlatl spears when Uncle Leno limped over to check my progress. Thinking about each kernel of corn having manitous, I asked, "Uncle Leno, do my fingernails have manitous, like kernels of corn?"

Without hesitation, he answered: According to teachings from our ancestors, they do. Everything Wisaka makes has a purpose, although the purpose may be difficult to comprehend; Because there are so many unknowns, Wisaka is often called ***a Trickster***. Kernels of corn are extra special because, in addition to food, they are seeds that keep corn alive for future generations; Regeneration of man and other creatures requires separate manitous to reproduce. Males need females, and females need males; That's also true with corn, acorns, and other growing things, although we don't understand how they mate;

Wisaka keeps secrets until we need to know; then He will provide enlightenment. Two of our greatest teachings are *(1) I AM A MESKWAKI AND I WAS CREATED OUT OF RED EARTH* and *(2) WISAKA HAS TAUGHT ME ALL I NEED TO KNOW, AND THAT IS ALL I NEED TO KNOW.* Our beliefs are based on our heritage and experiences; That's why Meskwakis think others' beliefs are good for them and our beliefs are good for us; Too many people know with certainty what they can't know, and that's why I disagree with French Jesuit priests;

Our fingernails die when torn off, and new ones can grow back. The location of our nail manitous' Happy Hunting Ground is a complete mystery to me; It's good that you think about and question ideas and things. I will tell you there's much we can never know. So don't worry too much about what you can't know; Otherwise you will spend most of your time worrying. You're better off doing something productive.

I didn't understand Uncle Leno's reasoning, yet felt sure this was wise advice. At least, I stopped pondering so much about the final resting places for various manitous.

§§§

Grandfather Nodin was our favorite storyteller. Other families and clans would ask him to join their fire circles. He stood and wildly moved around when it was his turn to tell a story. He would scare, tickle, teach, and entertain us. Often he would accomplish all of these feats in the same tale. Achak, our chief, would squirm when Nodin started telling things Achak did while trying to convince Anna to marry him. The rest of us including Anna would giggle and laugh. Good or favorite stories were repeated and seldom came out the same way. Nodin's way was to add lots of extra information to the smallest fact or story. By his face and demeanor, we understood when Nodin was stretching the truth to make his story more interesting or entertaining. When he passed along ancestors' words, he was a serious talker. Such was the case when he talked about my blue eyes.

Grandfather Nodin told us: When I was a youngster around fire circles like this one, my Meskwaki grandfather, Ahanu, told the family that a few of our early ancestors came from the north along the great eastern sea; They were warriors who could mate with our females like wolves mating with dogs. Their eyes were blue-or-greenish with hair the color of autumn maple leaves. That's why sometimes we have blue eyes in our families; Arriving in big canoes, they fought with long knives and axes. They called themselves Vikings and built a small village where they brought and kept animals with four teats. These animals were called cows who gave sweet milk. Our ancestors traded furs for some of this milk and red cloth.

Grandmother Wopk, a Mi̇̀kmaq and wife of Ahanu added to the story: A winter came that lingered a few full moons before turning into spring. The freezing weather and lack of food forced a group of Vikings to leave their village; They came up the large river that connects our great lakes with the eastern sea. They met and mated with some of our Beothuk ancestors, who helped them survive the winter; A scarred-face Viking learned enough of our talk to tell us in their land, four rivers of milk flowed from the teats of a magic cow. The Vikings believed there were four very strong people placed at the four corners of the World who hold it up. Their names were North, South, East, and West. This was long before the French, English, Spanish, and Dutch started swallowing our land and taking whatever they could load in their big ships. It was so long ago their eye coloring rarely shows up in their grandchildren who live in our land.[5]

When Anna heard this story, she would add: In my family, blue eyes are much closer; My mother's father, Nelson, was a Dutch trapper with blue eyes from New Amsterdam; His wife, my grandmother, Okeema was a Sauk; My sister, Meda, also married a blue-eyed Dutch trapper. So, Tyr's blue eyes show he could be a descendant of the Vikings or Dutch, both brave and adventuresome people.

Around seven winters, some teased me about the color of my eyes. Anna and others already had convinced me it was an honor to have Vikings or Dutchmen as early ancestors. Since my eyesight was excellent, I considered blue eyes a blessing.

§§§

One of Nodin's favorite fire circle stories was about ***thunderers.*** He would tell about thunderers who ride the winds from the south and are guardians against evil snakelike serpents with horns. They were called manetos—dangerous water panthers who lurk beneath the surface of large seas, lakes, and rivers. They would harm us if the thunderers didn't kill them with lightning strikes when they left the safety of deep water.

He then reminded us, "Wisaka created Earth and everything on or in it. Wisaka molded all people from red clay, and He called us his first and chosen children—*the Red Earth people*."

With an abundance of hand waving, body antics, and sounds, Nodin would continue: Since long ago, Grandfather

---

[5]Appendix B is a concise summary of Viking travels to Vinland, where they first met Red-Earth Beothuks or Mi'kmaqs—both Algonquian people. The Meskwaki Tribe (Red-Earth people) were longtime neighbors of the Mi'kmaqs along the St. Lawrence River. Definitions of Red-Earth people include the following meanings: 'My kin or we began from the same land.'

Thunder shoots lightning arrows into the evil monsters keeping them underground so his people can populate the Earth. Wisaka loves his people and creatures, especially us. You can tell by how he holds us close to Earth's bosom. If you jump up, he pulls you back. If you fall, you fall to Earth. For those that fly, he makes sure their home is in the trees or on the ground.

Grandfather Thunder served us so long our people only thought bad thoughts about his loud voice. Finally, these thoughts made him mad. From his southern home, he called out in a shake-the-earth voice. Then he shot lightning arrows, killing people, and burning things. The clouds cried large tears of sorrow. At first, he worked alone. After a time, his helpers came with him. Their rattles filled with bones shook the sky. This made our families fearful.

Wisaka knew we were in distress. He advised: Treat Grandfather Thunder with kindness and respect; When winter is over, and you hear him announce spring and awaken the Earth, you need to be thankful; And tell him so in your prayers and burn tobacco for him. Then his lightning arrows will not strike you while it rains for your crops; Meanwhile, Grandfather Thunder will keep shooting his lightning arrows at the evil monsters, keeping them underground, so they will not harm us.

Before my encounter with the *Storm from Hell*, I had heard this story several times. I noticed the absence of the story from our fire circles a long time after the experience. When I finally heard it again I asked, "Why did Grandfather Thunder hurt Machk, Tyr, and kill Ullich, Little Bear, Hasun, and Grey Wolf." Nodin's reply was: I know your question needs an answer. There are some questions to which we can't know the answers; We are left to wonder and guess. Perhaps our village people had forgotten the true importance of Grandfather Thunder, and he picked your group to voice his concern, or perhaps Ullich or others in the group had shown special disrespect for Grandfather Thunder; We know our understanding of manitous isn't perfect; Nevertheless, I and others believe in the fundamental truth about Kehci Manitou, Wisaka, and the relationship of all manitous. Countless forefathers have passed down this wisdom before us, and we shouldn't let a few events discourage the teaching of our long-held beliefs.

Other voices by elders around the fire circle supported Grandfather Nodin's explanation. I was still confused, but in the future, not taking a chance, I thanked Grandfather Thunder more often and burned a little tobacco for him.

§§§

A Jesuit Priest never visited our village, but our elders had met them at Meskwaki villages near Lake Winnebago. During a clan fire circle, the topic of Jesuit Priests and their use of Bibles led to a discussion on the value of learning to read and write words. Uncle Leno thought it would be wonderful if all people could speak, write, and read words in one common language. He was surprised at the intense disagreements from our Fox clan members.

The main arguments were: no written word would help us eat, sleep, grow, or harvest crops; find, kill, or cook our game, and on and on. We barely have enough time to take care of tasks and don't have the time to create, then learn to write, and read our own language.

If we learned to read and write a language already created, which language should it be? We detest the French and have few dealings with the English, Spanish, or Dutch.

So for us, learning to read and write is a wasted dream. It's like learning to fly like an eagle. The primary spokesperson for this position, was my mother, Anna—Uncle Leno's sister.

Not surprised, we had to listen to pros and cons in our lodge after the fire circle, until Uncle Leno finally said, “I am right for the future; you are right for the present.” Anna closed the conversation with, “You can live in the future; most of us have to live in the present!”

§§§

Aunt Wapun had long been a happy and productive adopted Meskwaki. A Chippewa, she spent her early childhood in a Chippewa village. There she learned about dream catchers. She and Uncle Etchemin had two children. Before each was born, she made them dream catchers. Later, most children in our village had dream catchers. About once a year Aunt Wapun would refresh our understanding of the history, purpose, and construction of dream catchers as follows:

An ancient Chippewa Legend tells us there was a great spirit named Spider Woman. Her magical webs caught babies' and children's dreams. She aimed Grandfather Sun's morning rays to burn and destroy bad dreams caught in her web. And she guided pleasant dreams through a small hole in the center of each web so babies and children only remembered pleasant dreams. The Chippewa Nation grew so large Spider Woman couldn't weave enough magical webs. Therefore, she directed grandmothers, mothers, and female family members to weave magical webs for their babies and children, using circular hoops made from willow limbs. The webs were woven with sinew and symmetrically anchored to the hoop in eight places representing the number of her spider legs. The circles represented Grandfather Sun's path around Earth. You can tie a feather near the center as a symbol of breath or air. Spider Woman called these dream catchers.

Aunt Wapun made a dream catcher for me. All my youthful dreams must have been bad and destroyed by this dream catcher because I have no recall of childhood dreams.

.

§§§

Nodin told us his *Mean Uncle Story*: I had an Uncle. Luckily, none of you ever met him. He was meaner than mean. He was a nasty man! All of us kids hated him and wished something bad would happen to his ornery soul. Well, one morning, he was out hunting birds in the woods, and a giant seven foot rattlesnake lay on a log. My uncle, whose eyes were pointed toward birds in the sky stepped over that log and was struck in a very private place by the poisonous snake. For several days, he suffered much pain and agony. Finally, finally (a very long pause by Nodin) *the rattlesnake died*!

We chuckled, then burst out laughing. Nodin fooled us and we liked to be fooled by friends. Humor was an important part of our lives.

§§§

Our lives were intertwined with birds, animals, fish, trees, water, plants, flowers, insects, and other wonders and dangers of Nature every day.

One afternoon, I was helping wash Anna's pots. A dirty vessel was about eight feet away, and a small lizard started to climb the side. He made it about halfway up, then slipped, falling back to the ground. The pot had a wider top than the bottom with walls tapering out. It had some leftover stew which attracted buzzing flies. These were the lizard's prey.

Once again, he began the climb, only to fall. Interested in the outcome, I continued to watch. He relentlessly started toward the top. Again the slippery sides of the pot and the loving pull of Earth conspired, and he fell. The fourth time he circled about a third of the way around and began a new assault; again he failed. One more time, he climbed from his most recent starting point with the same results.

Next, he turned and slithered up a nearby rock. I thought he had given up. Not this lizard, he leaped from his rock, almost grabbing onto the top edge of the pot, only to slip and fall. Again he slithered up the rock and made another leap from a slightly different spot. This time he hit the top edge and his momentum *flung him to the bottom of the pot.*

What determination, and what problem-solving ability. ***I stood and cheered***. The audience was Anna, the nearby creek, the forest, and thousands of little creatures within hearing distance. I turned the pot onto its side, so the victor could easily move onto his next adventure. While watching him snatch a few flies, he also tasted Anna's stew. Anna heard the cheer. When asked about the yelling, I told her the story. She said I should repeat it at the next fire circle, which I did.

After reciting the story, my friend Keme asked, "What did the lizard look like?" I told him it was black, had some stripes, and a dark blue tail. Next, he asked, "Did it have red on its chin or head?" "Nope," I replied. Then he said, "It's a good story, even though your 'hero' was a 'shero.'" Everyone laughed, including Anna who told us, "Always remember how important Nature is to our survival whether we are male or female."

Cheering a lizard's determination or holding my breath while watching a flock of robins swarm and strip a holly berry tree, I became a part of Mother Nature. The birds can accomplish this within seconds and then disappear in a wild musical whirr with all the trees' berries in their bellies. These small examples of Nature's magnificent enormity illustrate why we appreciate Nature and our way of life. Wisaka spiritually knitted everything on Earth together and each manitou is important.

During fire circles our elders reminded us Nature includes everything in the sky as well as what's on Earth, and *what happens in the sky can influence what happens on Earth.*

That's why Kehci Manitou's home is in the great White River of stars, and we spend a lot of time watching the sky. By the time most of us were eight winters, if we could see the Sun or North Star, we knew directions—north, south, east, west, and in between. Sky markers could be seen unless obscured by weather. If necessary, we could stay put until the weather cooperated and the sky was visible. As we aged, it became apparent the sun did not always rise or set precisely east or west. It was closest to east or west just two months out of the year—March and September.

We kept track of the moon and its phases. To us, the cycle started when the moon was full and ended when the moon was dark and unseen. This was called a dead moon. Often this was the night when the stars were the brightest.

Knowing the cycles helped us make the proper corrections to find true east and west during daylight hours, 12 months a year. Also, there are other ways, such as directions of tree growth, moss position, and shadows. With the sun, stars, moon, and other indicators an adult Meskwaki was never lost. I suspect, like your talker, most of them have been *temporarily confused* more than once.

Names for the 12 full-moon cycles:

January's full moon—The **Wolf Moon**, the snows gather in the deep woods, and howling wolves can be heard in the cold crisp air.

February's full moon—The **Snow Moon**, it's the heaviest snow month, which makes the tasks of walking and hunting more difficult.

March's full moon—The **Sap Moon**, the temperature warms, and maple tree sap begins to flow. That's when we start tapping the maple trees and making syrup, and sugar.

April's full moon—The **Pink Moon**, that's when pink, wild ground phloxes appear as a sign. Other flowers would soon begin to appear.

May's full moon—The **Corn Planting Moon**, that's when we plant our most important and life-sustaining crop.

June's full moon—The **Strawberry Moon,** is a favorite time for many. The weather is delightful, and strawberry picking, eating, and processing takes place.

July's full moon—The **Buck Moon**, new antlers of buck deer push out of their foreheads coated in velvety hair. Deer, like corn, make up large and important parts of our diet.

August's full moon—The **Green Corn Moon**, corn is so vital to Meskwakis that we name three full moons after its life cycle, planting, ripening green in the hot sun, and harvesting. Because of the reddish appearance of the moon through the sultry haze of August, some tribes call this *The* **Red Moon**.

September's full moon—The **Harvest Moon**, corn is harvested in September as well as pumpkin, beans, squash, and rice. About every five years, we harvest corn in October. At the peak of harvesting, this late rising and bright full moon allows harvesters to work late into the night.

October's full moon—The **Hunter's Moon**, occurs when fields are harvested and only the grain and stubble are left to attract deer, and other animals trying to fatten up for the winter. Leaves are falling, so game is easier to see Therefore, it's an excellent time for hunters to begin killing and storing meat for the long winter ahead.

November's full moon—The **Beaver Moon**, beavers are busy preparing for the winter. It's time to set beaver traps before the small streams and swamps freeze over. Beaver furs were needed both for personal use and swapping to fur traders for many different items that made our lives easier.

December's full moon—The **Cold Moon**, announces winter, our coldest season of the year, and it's also the last full moon of the year.

Because it revealed and helped so much, we spent a lot of time watching the sky and, as an entertaining bonus, saw a lot of shooting stars, and strange moving lights. Kehci Manitou never sleeps.

We discussed these subjects and many more at different times around our fire circles.

Beavers

"Why have beavers become so important?" Answering my question, Uncle Leno responded, "The white people must reproduce like ants to need so many beaver hats. Because of this, the beavers make many things good. For us, they make axes, knives, muskets, pots, feathers, and even fish hooks." At the time, we were cane pole fishing, and he was threading his line through a metal hook. The metal hooks were superior to our bone hooks. We disliked many white people. Nevertheless, they brought many useful things we liked and often decided we needed.

The mosquitoes were whining, and biting and I asked why Wisaka would create these horrible little creatures to torture his chosen people?

Uncle Leno said that when he was a young boy, mosquitoes didn't exist in our land. Along with muskets, metal fish hooks, and strange diseases, they arrived with the white people. Wisaka allowed this to happen. While mosquito noises and stings irritate, mosquitos have become an important part of the food chain. Birds eat mosquitoes, and mosquitoes lay their eggs in still water where fish, frogs, and turtles eat them. If we saw a wolf headed our way, we would forget about the mosquitoes. Mosquitoes' food-chain value must be more important than donating a few drops of blood. So they are a nuisance, not horrible.

Later, while helping Anna clean pots, I remarked, "Beavers made these pots." Anna asked, "What do you mean?" Repeating what Uncle Leno told me, she cleared her throat with her mouth closed, making a growling sound, meaning: *What a Bunch of Crap*. Our family had heard the sound before. I knew a vigorous rebuttal would follow. She asked, "Can Leno eat my pots?" I replied, "No, maybe there are enough beavers to feed us and get the things we need, or we could just eat deer, bear, or other game."

Anna's response made a lot of sense. She continued, "Wisaka is shedding great tears over rotting meat and our future without beaver meat. We are killing so many beavers it will not be long until beavers are as difficult to find around here as polar bears. It's easy to predict that soon we may have more pots with little meat to put in them."

Still, we kept killing beavers, and I kept making atlatls and spears for beaver skin payments, making our lives easier. Anna knew this, and she also thought 'horrible' was a better description of mosquitoes than 'nuisance,' and gave her loving brother credit for having thicker skin than most people.

Since our people can remember, they remember beavers and their ways. One reason is, like beavers, we stayed close to rivers, streams, and lakes. Equally important, they were a significant food source. Because they were plentiful, and easy to kill, we liked their taste, and as Uncle Leno said, "Their fur is so valuable we can trade it for whatever we need or want." Adult beavers weighed around 50 pounds and had large, sharp teeth, and flat tails.

According to one of our Meskwaki legends, learned around a fire circle, this is why they have flat tails.

Why Beavers Have Flat Tails

Once upon a time, there was a beaver who bragged about his bushy tail to a bird and a muskrat. Their insulting replies upset beaver. Mad, he returned to his dam and relieved his frustration by cutting down a large tree. As he was trimming, he kept thinking about his unappreciated tail and didn't notice he was cutting at a bad angle. The tree began falling toward him, and he jumped to get out of the way. He was too slow, and the tree flattened his beautiful tail. This made beaver sad, and he started to cry.

He heard a voice. It was Wisaka, who asked, “Why are you crying?” “A tree crushed my beautiful tail,” the beaver replied, “Now no one will like me.”

Wisaka told him, “We don’t like beavers for their tails, we like them for their kindness and wisdom. With your flat tail you can now swim faster and when you want to send a message to a friend, just slap your tail on the water.” This made beaver happy again. When the animals saw his flattened tail, they were shocked! Beaver announced, “It’s better this way.” After his discussion with Wisaka, the beaver never bragged about his tail, and other animals now liked him better.

That's how the beaver flattened and learned to like his tail.

§§§

To warn each other of danger, beavers slap their tails against the water, creating a loud splash. Other than people, beavers have few natural enemies. They spend most of their time in water, and can stay under water for about 20 minutes. When cornered on land, they rear up on their hind legs and hiss or growl. Then they lunge forward to deliver vicious bites with their axe-like teeth. When you hear them hiss and don’t have a weapon ready to kill them, your best action is to be somewhere else as fast as possible.

Left alone, they are independent, peaceful, and hard-working creatures—much like a Meskwaki. For several summers, Alawa, my sister, had a pet beaver named ‘Clever.’

Mated pairs of beavers live together for many winters. Litters of about four kits are born in the spring. The kits remain with their parents until they are about two summers old. Alawa met Clever when he was a newly weaned kit.

Clever's parents partially dammed a creek that emptied into the Kickapoo within a quarter mile of our village. Our elders decided it was worthwhile to keep tearing down the beavers' efforts to completely dam the creek. In return, we had a ready supply of firewood and, if needed, meat.

Beaver dams and lodges make it easy to identify their presence. They are vegetarians who can't see well. They have excellent hearing and do most of their moving on land around sunset or sunrise.

Clever was an excellent name for Alawa's pet. By the end of the second summer, Alawa and Clever were swimming together. Alawa groomed him, and added a stripe of red dye on the top of his head.

About halfway through the third summer, Clever disappeared. That's near the time beavers leave their family lodges, find a mate, and start their own family. For several summers, Alawa hoped she would see her pet again. Sadly, no one in our village ever saw Clever again.

To kill beavers, we (a paddler and a hunter) sometimes canoed five or six miles up the Kickapoo before the approach of night. We quietly let the canoe drift with the current. When dusk arrived, we stayed close to a bank. This is when beavers come ashore for food and wood, or mud required to repair their lodges. We seldom floated home without one or more dead beavers.

Before the arrival of white people, we would kill enough beavers to feed our families and try to save mating pairs, so kits wouldn't die of starvation and new kits could replenish the beaver family and help repair their lodge. Now beavers were being slaughtered at alarming rates, and our code of only killing what one needs to eat had been forsaken for European goods. *Anna knew what she was talking about.*

Keme, Village Hero

About dawn, Anna was usually first up in our lodge. If Nadi and Wapun weren't awake, she would wake them, and they would kindle the hearth fires and prepare food. To limit smoke in our lodge they would cook over the outside fire circle pit when weather permitted. Their noise or the aroma of morning meals woke the rest of us. Adult men were next on their feet, and children, eldest-to-youngest, were last.

One early-lazy morning, our family had finished eating when the eastern door rattled. Keme's Uncle Mukki yelled, "Achak, we need you out here! **Keme has killed a man**!" All uninvited males in our lodge quickly followed Achak out the door.

Mukki and Keme were kneeling over a warrior with his head smashed in. A blood-covered Keme didn't appear hurt, he just seemed dazed. Achak promptly declared, "We don't want a crowd out here. Mingan, you quietly ask the council members to come for a meeting." Then he asked, "Keme, what happened?" Keme wasn't too confused, since the following words were close to his nonstop reply:

You know the woods opposite the big bluffs? I decided to trot out there and back for a little exercise. As light approached, the trees were like shadows, and the dew was still heavy on the leaves and ground. It was so inviting I decided to wade the river and see if I could count coup on a deer:

Motionless next to a giant oak, I heard someone wade the river. It was a man slithering along from tree to tree and headed my way. I knew he wasn't a friend because I could smell him. With my club in hand, I hugged the tree, circling and hiding like a lizard. The intruder directly came to my tree with a warclub in hand. As he darted away, fearing for my life, I struck him in the head, smashing it like a pumpkin. He pitched sideways and lay there like a rock. I knew he was dead;

My first thought was to run to the village so no one would know I killed him. Then I rolled him over and noticed a tattoo was visible on his lower right jaw. Believing he was Iroquois, I decided to bring him in;

He was heavy. Still, I lifted him on my shoulders and stumbled to the village. I slipped on rocks wading the river and stopped to rest a couple of times.

By this time, council members had arrived, and Achak announced, "You are right, he is an Iroquois warrior, and I don't know why he would be here. Mukki make sure Keme is okay and feed him. There's food in our lodge. Tyr you stay with them. After the council talks, we want Keme to repeat his story and take a couple of trackers to the killing spot.

That's the last I saw the warrior or his belongings. He was removed from the village and buried with his possessions. The council heard Keme's story again. Achak and Uncle Leno agreed Keme's description was almost word-for-word, as told earlier. So, he had rehearsed the answer. Achak felt sure the Iroquois was ambushed and didn't have his war club in hand. He believed if Keme hadn't ambushed him then Keme would be dead. The level of rigor mortis confirmed Keme's timing, and the angle of the blow showed they were both upright, which meant Keme didn't ambush him when he was asleep.

A tattoo on the warrior's face was an eagle—his protective spirit. Marks on his war club showed he had killed or captured six enemies, and was wounded a couple of times himself. He had a wampum necklace. These were sometimes used as an agreement or message between two important chiefs. Our council believed this warrior was passing a message from a major Sioux chief to a major Iroquois chief and felt safer to travel by land than water.

Achak and Uncle Etchemin took the warrior's war club and wampum necklace to Chief Pemoussa, located on high ground south of Big Lake Butte Des Morts. Achak reported the circumstances to Chief Pemoussa, who believed it was bad news for our Meskwaki Tribe.

A small village ceremony honored Keme, now a village hero, for killing an important enemy warrior.

Favorite Game

During winters, the beaver pond routinely froze over, and the older boys would build large fires on the bank next to each end of the pond and play my favorite game called nighttime ice shinny. This pond was the same one where Alawa discovered her friend—Clever. The beavers learned our ice shinny games were temporary distractions. Two of the older boys would be game chiefs. When I first played, Mingan was often one of the game chiefs, and I would be in his black kinship group.

In our ice shinny games, each player found their own slapping stick, which had to be a piece of wood. Most of the sticks came from the nearby beaver dam. A small chunk of charred wood was our game puck.

Each team had a fire line to guard. To score goals, the puck had to cross an imaginary line aligned with the center of the opponent's fire. Other than the moon and stars, these large fires were the only light. The fires were built just before dark.

The puck was centered on the ice between the two fires. Our game chiefs both had their sticks touching the puck. Their respective teams lined up across their own imaginary lines marked by the fires. On a signal, the two game chiefs started the puck whacking.

Many nights the moon was high in the sky before we finished. The time was spent sliding, shoving, blocking, screaming, swinging at the puck, and being knocked or falling down. Then, picking ourselves up from the ice until vertical and repeating the process over again. Time outs were only allowed for injuries, putting more wood on the fires or arguing over tripping, and hitting-with-stick claims or scores.

One night, the chunk of charred wood stopped near the side of the pond where the light was flickering low. Mingan was close by. He skidded up to it. At the same instant he drew his club back, an owl swooped down and grabbed the puck. Without hesitation, Mingan finished his swing, and the owl became a puff of feathers. Both white and black players cheered, and Mingan took a bow. *I was proud of my big brother.*

The games were wild affairs. Our rewards were bruises and strained body parts. No matter how cold the weather was or how exhausted we were, we survived and had great fun. I loved this game. All the players loved the game. The games ended if one of the game chiefs yelled 'surrender' or we burned the gathered wood until we couldn't see, or the scorekeeper ordered us to put out the fire and go to sleep. When that happened, the scores were tabulated, and the winner was determined. A senior warrior, freezing on the sidelines, was our scorekeeper. There were never many onlookers at the start of a match, and only a few shivering souls usually stayed until we finished.

Meskwakis were taught to retreat if it was wise, but never surrender, so the duration of each game was determined by the size of the wood pile we gathered before each match. My favorite targets were Keme and Chaska, and they weren't hard to find because they took turns searching for and knocking me down.

We were aware of a rough contact game called Lacrosse, where players on each side would throw a small wooden ball with sticks having a cup on one end. Their target was a pole marked with scoring areas. Only villages with lots of players, and large playing fields, like the Chippewas, played full scaled Lacrosse. Their games would last from sun up to sun down. Ice shinny was our small-village winter substitute.

Repeatedly, Mingan provided tips on how to gain an edge in games or war. An example was to make sure the sun was at your back. For my favorite game, his advice was to anticipate where the puck was going and swing hard when you were close. The next objective was to knock down as many white guys as possible. We sometimes played a fair weather version of shinny.

Still, playing at night was more fun, and it was safer to fall on ice than on rocky ground.

Later as an ice shinny game chief, I repeated Mingan's advice. We had other village games. Most were competitive such as corn cob fights, races, wrestling matches, shooting arrows, throwing spears, knives, and war clubs at targets. They were all fun. We made games out of swimming, diving, climbing, canoeing, and other activities. Slinging atlatl spears was lots of fun, but I took spear slinging too serious. Ice shinny was my favorite game!

Vision Quest

To be called a man in our village, we had to complete a Vision Quest, which meant spending four days fasting alone in the forest, searching for our spiritual self. My non-spiritual self thought it was a foolish requirement. No matter; I wanted to be called a man. In early spring, after my thirteenth winter, I asked Achak if I could complete the quest, and he thought I was ready and would arrange it with Eluwilussit—our village Medicine man.

Chaska, Keme, and I called our Medicine man 'Elu;' but never to his face. While we had exchanged greetings, I had never talked with him.

Keme had completed his vision quest, so he met Elu. Keme wouldn't tell either of his friends anything, other than, "You'll find out." He considered the Vision Quest an important and mysterious event, and there was no way he would spill any of the beans, not even to his best friends.

Our medicine man was important and frequently spoke or chanted at village gatherings. When I encountered him, he always seemed in deep thought and seldom made eye contact.

Several days later, Achak advised, "Go to Eluwilussit's lodge, and he will tell you what's needed to complete your Vision Quest."

With trepidation, I went to Elu's lodge and tapped on his hanging-open door. A clear, happy voice ordered, "Tyr, come on in!" Surprised at the warm greeting, I quickly entered. His lodge was smaller than ours, with benches on both sides. There was a single fire pit, and its overhead opening exposed plenty of light. He motioned to take a seat directly opposite where he was sitting. *That was the only place to sit.* All other surfaces were covered with plants, powders, dead flower petals, seeds, feathers, hide pouches, pots, birch boxes, skulls, bear claws, and more. Additional clutter was hanging from the side walls and overhead frames. Anna and my aunts would have organized this mess in a hurry. Elu lived alone and apparently didn't worry about his lodge's appearance. The odor, while strange, was pleasant.

Elu's voice was relaxing; I quickly felt at ease. He congratulated my atlatl prowess, then asked, "What's your favorite bird?" My response "Eagle," "Favorite flower?" "Violet," "Favorite tree?" "Maple," and "Favorite animal?" I couldn't decide between a buffalo or a black bear. Elu said that my choices were fine. He was surprised about the choice of violets. I responded, "A violet was my first vivid memory and I still believe they are beautiful. Anna gathers them to make hot tea that helps cure fevers and aches." Elu replied, "A good mind works that way, and your Vision Quest should help make clear your favorite animal, who will be your spiritual soul mate."

Continuing, he said, "You know you aren't supposed to smoke tobacco until you've killed a rabbit, a deer, and a buffalo before becoming a man." I admitted, "Yes, I know. I've smoked a few times. I've killed a number of rabbits and deer. But, no buffaloes. Anna smelled my smoking breath a couple of times and had Achak throw me in the Kickapoo. I gave it up. Extra baths were okay. Smoking tobacco wasn't worth the trouble."

Elu's lips didn't smile, although his eyes did. Aunt Nadi claimed that if you want to know what people actually think, watch their eyes closer than you listen to their words. Then Elu declared, "You're lucky; Anna and Achak know what's best."

He finished the session by reviewing the complete process: Your Vision Quest will start with an early morning cleansing session in the sweat lodge; next, you will take a short swim in the coldest water where the big spring enters the creek. Then you will spend four days alone in the forest. During this time you must fast, so eat a good breakfast, and drink plenty of water before your cleansing. The purpose of the quest is to meet and better understand your manitou. Mostly hidden, it's an important part of your life; To aid your quest, I will mix a powder of jimson weed and add crushed morning glory seeds. You must combine this powder with water and drink it. This drink will make you temporarily dizzy. Also, it should help free your mind, making it easier to become acquainted with your manitou; Your choice of location should be isolated from villages at a place safe and appealing to you. You need to take a medicine pouch for saving things that seem sacred, a sleeping blanket, and your knife; Take your atlatl and axe in case you need to protect yourself or build a shelter; When you return, we will meet and discuss the results of your quest. If it's successful, we will celebrate around your Fox Clan fire pit, where you will leave your boyhood behind and become a man.

This happened as Elu directed. I chose Wildcat Mountain because high places give me a sense of wonder and freedom. It is the highest point overlooking the Kickapoo River.

After an early morning cleansing and a cold swim, I fast-walked to Wildcat Mountain. Before dark, there was time to climb the mountain. Skirting along the western top, I found an excellent place to search for myself.

Previously, Keme, Chaska, and I visited this mountain a few times. Here we watched a strange flight of two eagles. They were first seen high over the mountain top and the Kickapoo. They flew at each other, then away several times, as if playing high-altitude tag. Then, from on high, they locked their claws together and started an unbelievable tumble toward the river. Stuck together, they cartwheeled, flipped, and dropped until they almost hit the Kickapoo, where they parted, and quickly regained their lost altitude. We later learned we had witnessed an eagle wedding ceremony. This was another reason I chose the mountain, I hoped to see a repeat performance of an awesome show. It didn't happen.

When one is fasting, finding food is not a problem. The chosen campsite was near a small bubbling spring and safely away from the mountain's edge. No large trees were obstructing the western view, and several small ferns and assorted brush were in the way. With axe and knife, soon the westward wide-open spaces were visible. Beneath a large pine tree, fern leaves and pine needles made a soft place to sleep. It was dry and no shelter was needed. The spring air had a slight chill, so a campfire was next. Downed pine and hemlock trees were scattered nearby, making this another simple task. A few rocks were promptly gathered, and soon a brisk fire was blazing.

There was enough time before sunset to drink the trance powder. On my knees, I dumped the powder into the small mixing container. Then spread the bear robe on the soft bedding material and propped myself in a siting position, back against the pine tree.

Forest creatures will come near, when it's still and quiet for a while. Some squirrels began scolding the intruder from a nearby pine. Ignoring their insults, I wrapped myself in the bear robe, closed my eyes for a quick rest, dozed off, and didn't wake until sunset. This was the excuse needed to put off drinking the trance maker until tomorrow.

Interrupting the sun's dimming glow, a big black panther silently floated across the newly chopped clearing. It was like watching a black log floating down a stream, except it was gone, almost before being seen. Did I really see a panther up close and with no sound? Under these strange circumstances, I wasn't sure. Had I consumed the powder? No, the powder was in the mixing container. It was covered to keep the powder dry.

Although confused, I knew Tyr was staring in the precise direction of the Happy Hunting Ground, where hopefully, my spirit, the subject of this quest would spend eternity.

The next memory was a screaming noise. Now wide awake, the fire was blinking embers, and there was light from a half-moon and sky full of stars. Hearing the scream again, it was close and sounded like a woman screaming, similar to a panther's mating call. The sound and chill running down my spine were proof enough. I had seen a black panther!

Blowing on the embers and adding some kindling and a couple more logs to the fire, I snuggled in the bear robe and awoke before sunrise, thirsty, and hungry as a bear. With the morning sun's warmth, I quit stalling. The medicine man's order was to mix the powder in the container of water thoroughly. I added water to the powder and stirred, stirred, shook it all around, and stirred some more, then gulped it down in two swallows.

Thinking there would be a quick reaction, I waited and waited. Finally giving up, I started to stand. Dizzy! I couldn't get up. The world was spinning. Somehow sick and spinning faster than the world, I managed to crawl to the mountain's edge and puke poison. Standing, I spread my arms and dived. Floating downward, I inhaled air all the way to my little toes. The black panther was below. Purring he caught Tyr on his back and carried me back to the mountaintop. *Screaming thanks*, I picked him up, all seven or eight feet, and tossed him off the mountain, then followed him into the abyss. Down, down we went like two eagles in heat. Passing through each other, I became one with the panther until he softly dropped me into the river.

This was a wonderful place and the perfect time for a little dip in the Kickapoo. Landing in a whirlpool, its enticing arms held and wooed me while breathing air from my little toes. Tiring of the pleasure, I swam laterally, like brother Mingan had taught me to escape a whirlpool. That's when I saw the water monster—a scary panther-like creature with horns, scales, and a tail like a fish.

With Wisaka's help, the whirlpool lifted me to the surface and hurled me to the mountaintop. Now reclining on my

Vision Quest bed and surrounded by a field of violets, I watched the black panther start my fire, then sit next to me, and stare deep into my eyes. Penetrating my soul, he said, “My friend, you are weird and have blue eyes like mine.”

Later, I awoke warmly wrapped in my bear robe. There were no violets. The fire was burning, and Tyr had a sore throat from a dream of screaming like a panther. Where was a dream catcher when needed?

The sun was about the same place in the sky when I arrived yesterday. Or did I arrive yesterday and spend more than half-of-a-day recovering from the influence of jimson weed and morning glories? The rest of the day was spent trying to sort fact from fiction. The next day and night my memories were hunger pains and how difficult it was to stay away from food and, especially, the bubbling spring.

On the final morning, when rolling up my bear robe for return to the village, I found two small black shiny pebbles, each about the size of my thumb. The stones were not there when the bear robe was placed. I already owned a similar stone, found earlier in a deep cave close to the mouth of the Kickapoo. It was in my medicine pouch, along with a few other trinkets. Even more puzzled, the two new pebbles were added to my pouch. Sorting out facts wasn’t easy. It was impossible.

What’s reported here is what happened, as I remembered. They were unbelievable, drug induced dreams. Who could make up such weird experiences? I had never seriously questioned our spiritual ideas. On some level, I thought they were happy, make-believe. I came away from the Vision Quest having a deeper appreciation for spiritual concepts and mysteries beyond one’s conscious comprehension. In addition, I gained a better understanding of why others may embrace those ideas with complete trust. In a way, this experience was similar to my encounter with the *storm from hell,* where my fear was so great it caused my manitou to shut down reality until I could handle it.

At a minimum, my Vision Quest was convincing enough that my spiritual guide became a blue-eyed black panther. A choice that later helped me through some tough times.

I came away with a complete *lack of understanding* of how I could find small black pebbles, wake up with a wet body, a sore throat, and a blazing fire while never leaving the mountaintop. One lesson I learned was wanting nothing else to do with putting jimson weed and morning glories in my mouth.

§§§

Eluwilussit listened to my story and concluded, "You had a productive Vision Quest, and your blue-eyed black panther is an excellent choice for your protective spirit. After our celebration of your successful vision quest, you can smoke tobacco without Achak tossing you in the Kickapoo."

At my Vision Quest celebration, Aunt Wapun replaced my shoddy medicine pouch with a soft, handsome deerskin one. I never forgot dear Aunt Wapun or the strange out-of-my-world Vision Quest.

Sex in the Village

One doesn't live in the close quarters of a crowded lodge and near animals without learning about mating. Little verbal instruction is needed. I was about eight winters before I understood mating was how an animal made babies and my PeePee had another function besides relief and watering plants, and trees. Later, I learned this was called 'having sex' and other names.

Many of our girls were married by the time they were fourteen winters. This was encouraged. More babies helped increase our chances of survival. In our tribe and village, the sanctity of marriage was important and included the practice of polygamy. Some successful warriors or chiefs had more than one wife, and often they were sisters or cousins of the first wife. There was no polygamy in our lodge.

On a gorgeous spring morning, I couldn't concentrate on atlatl work. Chaska was busy doing other tasks. I was alone. The sun was a yellow orb smiling from its low eastern perch through a sky filled with small, medium, and large smokey-white clouds, all slowly gliding east-north-east in near-perfect sync across the light-blue sky. A slight refreshing breeze was like touch-music telling me to enjoy the scene. Not one to resist such temptation, I laid back on a soft grassy spot and considered how easy it would be to jump from one cloud to the next. Earlier atop several different mountains, I had thrust my hand into low clouds and knew they were like fog—just air saturated with moisture. From a distance and in my state of mind, it looked like the clouds could easily hold my weight. Lazily, I began plotting a cloud trail across the sky.

This mind game was interrupted by the realization that music seemed to be coming from multiple directions. The birds were chirping in rhythm with the breeze-fed rustling of leaves and branches. The river was making harmonious ripple sounds; even beetles seemed to be clicking in time.

My noise reverie was interrupted by the chattering of a group approaching along the river bank. Getting off my reclined butt, I grabbed an atlatl and pretended to be busy. From a distance and my elevation, it looked and sounded like a moving flower garden, making sounds of happiness similar to the chirping birds. A yellow butterfly was flitting around a group of flowers headed my way.

The garden was more than a dozen young girls. They had ribbons, mostly red, in their hair. The butterfly had a large yellow ribbon in her hair. Climbing the river bank and stopping to watch the atlatl guy, the butterfly, who seemed to be the oldest girl, flitted to the front of the crowd. I had met the lady leading them and knew she was Elyshia's Aunt Kanti, the medicine man's helper. I had seen Elyshia around the village and knew her name. Unfortunately, 'Big Mouth' was flustered, and not thinking of anything better to say, I asked, "What's your name?"

She tilted her head, directed soft brown eyes straight into mine, and replied, "**Elyshiiiiia** and I know yours, it's Tyr!" Peeved that I didn't know her name, she continued, "You're the boy who wastes time playing with atlatls. Atlatls are outdated. Muskets and bows and arrows are better." Her hands waved as she talked. She opened both hands, palms up, showing it was my turn to speak. "Yes, it is kind of dumb," I mumbled while thinking, what's really dumb is that I froze and couldn't remember her name. She was about one winter younger than the atlatl dummy and already wiser. While upset, she wasn't angry. It was more like Uncle Leno making someone aware of an important point.

I asked, "***Elyshia***, would you like to try slinging a few outdated atlatl spears?" Before she answered, her Aunt said, "Tyr is busy, and we need to finish our study of riverside plants." Elyshia pleaded, "Just once, Aunty?" Her Aunt didn't say a word, she nodded yes and stuck up one finger.

The target was about 35 feet away. I pointed at it and, showing off, planted a spear close to the center of the target. There was no sound from the unimpressed audience. Next, I showed Elyshia how to grip my atlatl, put it in her hand, and attach a spear. Then placed her finger around the spear and told her that she had to let loose quickly at the end of her throw. Then I stepped back and showed a casting motion with a strong flip at the end. Instantly, she said, "You mean like this!" With no other instruction, she launched the spear straight at the target. It was low and clipped the bottom of the target, directly below my spear. She threw it hard enough that it stuck quivering in the tree trunk. I was amazed and stunned. The girls screamed approval and my heart quivered like the spear. This pretty, skinny, budding-curves-in-the-right-places girl, full of life, and self-confidence, simply said, "Thanks." She handed me the atlatl, and the flower garden continued its journey up the river.

As I watched, the now *beautiful* butterfly resumed flitting around the other flowers, leaving me with a strange and special feeling. Little did she know how often I would manage to *accidentally* meet her. Having touched Elyshia, the wonderful surroundings were forgotten. Her confidence, energy, looks, and something more captured a heart. Sex was on my mind.

Thankfully, Elyshia belonged to the Bear Clan. It was taboo to have sex with anyone in your clan. That's one of the ways our people avoided the idiot-children negativity of incest. Most tribes we contacted had clans. A first question when meeting someone new was, "What's your Clan?" Not sure how many different clans there were in other tribes. Our Meskwaki Tribe had about 10—Buffalo, Elk, Deer, Fox, Bear, Eagle, Hawk, Sturgeon, Thunder, and Bass. More important to me, in our village, there were only five—Fox, Wolf, Sturgeon, Hawk, and Bear. A number of them were Fox. So my village-sanctioned sexual partners were limited. Sometimes a male clan member could marry a female of the same clan. Before such a marriage could occur, the clan's senior females had to evaluate their respective family lineages and approve the match. Senior clan members had other responsibilities, including enforcement of clan rules like the strict prohibition against adultery.

The French first met a hunting party of our Meskwaki brothers about 1665. Their first question was, "What's your tribe's name?" Not fully understanding and relying on tradition, our hunters answered, "Fox." The French, thinking our tribe's name was "Fox," renamed us Les Renards or the Foxes. The French spread this name to other colonists. To the outside reading world, the French first renamed us. Then later they attempted to chase our manitous to the west of the setting sun.

Your talker is not wise enough to provide sexual advice and would not provide information about sexual encounters or gossip in our village. Even though it was long ago, their manitous might still be listening, and I am wise enough to know how foolish that would be. Some topics are best kept private between individuals. While instruction and experience can be helpful, sex can best be enjoyed by two people who care for each other, experimenting, and learning together.

Thankfully, a third-party teacher normally isn't needed to learn how to breathe or propagate this sexually transmitted miracle we call ***life***.

Maple Syrup

There were thousands of sugar maple trees near the Kickapoo River. Maple syrup and maple sugar were staples of our diet. We put maple sugar on fruits, vegetables, and fish. Children were coaxed to take their medicine by adding a little maple sugar. The sugar was mixed with cold spring water for a welcome drink on a hot day and with hot water to make an equally welcomed cold-winter-day drink. Maple syrup and sugar were important trade items.

Processing maple sap into syrup and sugar involved intense labor. Able members of families, including children, joined to complete the tasks. It was difficult work. With the family together, it was also a time of fun and celebration. *This process was a necessary family and village tradition*.

The sap started to move down the trees during the third full moon, called the Sap Moon. Cold nights and warm days caused it to flow freely.

This upcoming season was going to be extra special. We had accumulated enough metal kettles to replace our birch bark boiling containers. The birch containers couldn't take direct flames, so we had to keep heating rocks and immersing them in the sap. It takes about 40 gallons of sap to make a single gallon of maple syrup. So dropping hot rocks into the birch containers to keep the sap boiling required a lot of messy drudgery.

No maple grove was large enough to supply syrup for the number of families in our village. Our elders claimed several groves as our village's *sugar camps*. The groves were different sizes and clan and family sizes were constantly changed. So each maple syrup season, one's immediate family would be together. The other families sharing a sugar camp were often different. This was fine. Shifting families kept our village more like one big family. I didn't know or care how the elder women figured it out. Amazingly, the spring after I met Elyshia, her family, my family, and Chaska's family shared the same sugar camp. New boiling kettles and rubbing elbows with Elyshia for several weeks would be an extra-sweet combination.

Although we had new kettles, the other equipment and process remained the same. The boiling sap still had to be tended, so it didn't burn. It was considered done when the boiled sap hung in thick strings from the stirring paddle. When the maple syrup was ready, some of it was strained and stored. Most of it was made into maple sugar blocks. There was no easy way to keep syrup, while dried and hardened maple sugar was easily made into sugar blocks and stored for later use or trade.

The maple syrup had to undergo additional boiling to eliminate water and make sugar. After it was strained and worked by hands to make granulated sugar, it was packed into molds to make small sugar cakes. A gallon of syrup made about eight pounds of sugar. Each maple tree we tapped, along with lots of labor, made about a half-gallon of maple syrup and took several days of sap flowing to drain the tree.

Snow was still on the ground when we headed to our sugar camp. Work was divided between the families when they arrived at the camp. Men and boys put the camp in good shape by repairing wigwams, clearing brush, and handling the heavy lifting. Sugar-making fires burned for many days, requiring a large stockpile of wood. The males also provided fish and game for the meals.

Women were the maple syrup and sugar chiefs. Aunt Wapun was the main chief. They planned, directed, and controlled each activity. Tapping about 200 trees, draining, and catching the sap, transferring it to boiling stations, keeping the fires burning, stirring, and monitoring the boiling sap, processing syrup to sugar, packing syrup and sugar for use and storage, teaching youngsters, and keeping everybody safe was a major project.

Uncle Etchemin reminded me, as he did every year, how lucky he was. This was because he only had to put up with Tyr during the Sap Moon, while poor Leno had to put up with me during all the remaining days. He would finish with a friendly shove to my closest shoulder. Uncle Etchemin was a patient teacher, with a ready smile and the gleam of friendship in his eyes. Among his many skills, he, like his wife Wapun, was a maple-syrup making expert.

Uncle Etchemin asked, "Sap Buddy, What's up? In the past, you've stuck to me like a leach; now you are invisible." I quickly replied that this season, I wanted to learn more about boiling sap, making sugar, and helping Chaska. His response, "Yeah, your interest in making sugar is called ***Elyshia***" This was followed by a friendly shove, knocking me down. Laughing, he helped me up, and declared, "Elyshia is a winner and far more important than being my shadow."

After all the maple syrup and sugar were loaded into birchbark storage containers, the women reported we had made a record amount with much less work. They were thrilled, which made the rest of us happy. Anna was pleased with the kettles, and no one reminded her how many beaver-skins the kettles cost.

Elyshia and I started the sap season as good friends and left as great kissing friends. We had to be close, exploring each other in the bitter cold. At least we were close when she wasn't busy with sugar work. I was surprised to learn from Elyshia that her young sister Chepi had a crush on, and was seeing Chaska.

Our families seemed happy that we were all such good friends. With loaded canoes, we had a chilly and challenging trip upstream to the village. Fighting the current and icy headwind, I paddled hard. Warmed by inner bliss, paddling wasn't that bad.

Horseless Buffalo Hunts

Hunting, killing, and processing a downed buffalo isn't easy and can be dangerous. Killing them for food and improving our lives was well worth the risk and strenuous work. They travel in herds. On the plains west of the Mississippi River, the herds were huge compared to those in the nearby meadows of our woodlands.

The herds near our Kickapoo River village seldom numbered more than 30 animals. These small herds broke from the larger ones and usually swam the Mississippi River from the west. As the crow flies, the distance from our village to the Mississippi River was about 15 miles. This distance is blocked by broken bluffs and mountains, interspersed with interlocking valleys. Some valleys open into other valleys through narrow pathways, while others lead to a dead ends. The valley networks are bound together by streams fed from springs, rain, melting snow, and watershed from surrounding hills, bluffs, and mountains. Besides grass, bushes, and low-hanging branches for food, a buffalo needs about 20 gallons of water a day. This necessity keeps them happily grazing along these stream-laced valleys.

Buffaloes are seldom aggressive, except during rutting seasons when bulls compete for mating rights or defend their offsprings or themselves. Because they don't eat meat and are large, and tough-skinned, they don't have to be aggressive. Bulls can weigh up to 2000 pounds, which is about twice the weight of their nearest competitor—a grizzly bear. Man is their only serious life-threatening danger besides the lack of food or water or Nature outbursts such as floods, fires, freezes, earthquakes, and droughts.

Their sense of smell is excellent, and their hearing is good. They are near-sighted. Each herd has a leader, commonly an old cow. Wherever she goes, the others follow. When she stampedes, they stampede. When she becomes confused, she mills around. The herd blindly follows, so they all mill around too. In this sense, buffaloes are dumb as stumps.

On a late summer day, Keme, Chaska, and I watched a herd of about 20 buffaloes in a valley below our bluff-side perch. One of the bulls strayed about 300 feet from the main herd. Without warning, a grizzly bear came loping out of nearby woods. Since he was downwind, the grizzly surprised the young-but-big bull, who quickly turned and started running toward the herd with his short tail erect like a huge scorpion.

The grizzly, having momentum, caught and leaped on the bull's back. The bear's claws couldn't hold on because the bull's body was too big. And the grizzly couldn't sink his teeth into the bull, because the skin was too tough. Shaking him off, the bull turned his horns toward the bear. Meanwhile, the herd slowly sauntered toward the standoff. Realizing he had tried to kill something he couldn't bring down, the grizzly retreated to the timber. The bull had claw marks on his back. He kept grazing as if nothing had happened.

We knew our villagers rarely hunted buffaloes until after the *Hunter's Moon* in the fall, after our crops are harvested and the buffaloes are fatter.

The patchwork of bluffs, hills, valleys, and streams provided many places to trap small buffalo herds. There was a stream that emptied into the Mississippi River about 20 miles north of Prairie du Chien. This stream attracted buffaloes swimming across the Mississippi like bees to honey. The stream was largely fed by a big spring in a dead-end valley five miles from our village. For us, this was an ideal killing site.

We kept this buffalo path inviting by torching, as needed, the interconnecting valley meadows after our fall buffalo killing and before winter set in. We blocked interfacing valley entrances where we wanted buffaloes to bypass.

Our kill site was an open-ended corral made of wood. Nearby our hunters hid out of sight until the buffaloes were herded into the corral. The first shot was an arrow into the herd's leader, who either went down or milled about in confusion. Either way, the followers didn't know what to do except mill around. Then, we launched arrows and spears at the trapped buffaloes. This mill-around-the-leader instinct made it easier to kill millions of buffaloes.

Three want-to-be-buffalo hunters, Keme, Chaska, and me, at one time or another shared in all of the aforementioned duties.

Together, our last horseless buffalo hunt followed the sequence of events covered. Each of our roles in the last hunt was killing. Chaska and I hurled atlatl spears from opposite sides of the corral while Keme shot arrows. Then Keme, with a hatchet in hand, scrambled over the corral fence with other adult males and finished the killing.

Chaska and I were ordered to stay out of the corral. I didn't care. This was a mindless slaughter. Still, it was satisfying to know our families would have food, and we would gain useful items furnished by buffaloes.

We killed 32 buffaloes. Before all the buffaloes were killed, our heavy lifters, including Keme, began dragging them out, one at a time and the butchering teams, including Chaska and me, went to work.

To reduce transportation weight, the butchers stripped the meat, leaving the bones (except those needed to make tools) near the killing site. Since our corral was close to the village, not much cooking was done at the site. We would cook and celebrate later at the village, and finish butchering and processing the meat and hides.

If we worked hard, we could return to the village before dark. We worked feverishly. There was cutting and slashing of carcasses; buffalo blood mixed with workers' sweat decorated most of us. There was shouting, quarreling, and laughing. The tired butchers, while cutting, would slice off and eat pieces of raw livers, kidneys, or other morsels or crack the big marrow bones, for the nutritious marrow.

Our women were in complete charge of every activity as soon as we killed the buffalo. It didn't matter who made the kills or whose roles were the most important. When we carried the meat and body parts to the village, a group of women representing each clan would do the sorting and distribution. They ensured the ill, crippled, old, and each family received a fair share. The women, along with their other duties, had the time-consuming, backbreaking work of drying and processing the meat. They also turned the hides into robes, clothing, and other items. In addition they prepared the jerky and pemmican. The only jobs left for the men were heavy lifting, and making tools or useful items from the bones.

About 100 Meskwakis, each shouldering loads, made the trek home. We were a tired, hungry, and happy bunch strung out over the trail to the village. A couple of runners dispatched to the village had fires burning in the fire pits when we arrived. Knowing our celebration and buffalo feast were about to begin, lightened the loads.

We left a large expert cleaning group behind. Their names included wolves, foxes, coyotes, badgers, raccoons, and birds. When they finished, there would be little left other than a few large bones. They went to work when we were out of bowshot range. Nature helped us in countless ways.

Our descendants may find the following-detailed list of buffalo parts used by our village of little interest. For us, it underscores why buffaloes were life-and-death important for our plains' cousins and almost as important for those of us raised in the woodlands.

Meat—Several hundred pounds of edible meat were harvested from each buffalo. Some of the meat was processed into jerky (air-dried, thin strips of meat) and pemmican (mixture of jerky pounded or ground into a meal-like consistency with berries and melted fat.)

Hide—Robes, bedding, moccasins, cradles, clothes, bags, quivers, drums, pouches, dolls, and wrapping the dead.

Sinew—Ropes, cords, bindings, sewing thread, and bow strings.

Intestines—Water bags, storage containers, and sausage making.

Hair—Pillows and rope.

Tail—Brushes and insect swatters.

Hoofs—Glue and rattles.

Horns—Cups, spoons, tools, and toys.

Brains—Tanning hides.

Gristle—Glue and baby teething.

Bones—Needles, awls, and tools such as digging hoes.

Bladder—Tobacco pouches and water containers.

Stomach—Storage or water containers.

Much later, I participated in many buffalo hunts that included horseback riding.

Those hunts, which involved stampeding herds, required skill, and a fear of danger that made one feel more like a proud hunter.

Mississippi River Adventures

Mississippi River Prelude

Similar to a light mist, the morning dew penetrated the canopy of cottonwood and willow trees where I slept next to the Kickapoo. Sleep had been fitful. Still tired, I wanted to lie there and do nothing.

An already-bright sun was peeking through the branches. The sun, hungry growls from my belly, river sounds, and a coat of dew all shouted, "Get up! Get up!" These are the sparks that light my fire. Forgetting tired, I sprang to my feet, fully awake.

The curvature of the bank and river formed a pond-like surface, and the sun and Kickapoo held hands to make a mirror. This mirror reflected the shore, the trees, and the rocks like identical twins staring at each other. I looked at myself in the scene and saw a muscular six-footer with broad shoulders, developed from hard work and play. The blue eyes with a tint of green seemed to smile no matter what mood I tried to convey by twisting my face around. My nose was too big, and my face was too wide to be handsome. Still, I realized that Wisaka was kind enough to mold this young guy into a good-looking dab of red clay. I was pleased with the image and happy to have blue eyes.

"UGLY, UGLY, don't you think?" The voice of Keme jolted my self-admiration into embarrassment. My knife was in hand, so I stroked the invisible stubble on my chin, and informed Keme and Chaska, who was grinning by Keme's side, that unlike them I needed to chop hair off my face. Splashing a handful of river water for lubrication, I quickly peeled off a hint of facial hair. Chaska mockingly added, "Yeah, and you had to do all that blinking and jaw-twisting just to find it." **We** laughed! When together, Keme, Chaska, and Tyr laughed a lot.

Earlier, when I told Keme about my Mississippi River plan, he insisted, “I have to go too. Without an expert guide, you’ll be lost before Rock River.” It was a relief to be joined by Keme for his help and added security. It was an extra special bonus when Chaska told us, “You brutes can’t leave without your brains, so I have to come along too!” Chaska’s parents provided their blessing.

There were reasons for this trip. I wanted a break from village rules, and was tired of making atlatls and spears. The death of my brother, Mingan, was another reason.

As Aunt Meda had warned, several Meskwaki chiefs led by Chief Pemoussa accepted France’s offer and moved almost 1,000 villagers (including brother Mingan) close to Ft. Pontchartrain, where war erupted. Most of our people were killed. Before the main battle, some left and joined the Senecas, and after the battle a few escaped. ***The results sent anger, rage, and fear racing throughout the remaining Meskwaki villages and the villages of our closest allies.*** My family’s first question was, ‘What happened to Mingan?’ We soon learned he was killed. Sharing the sad mourning routine, we each handled it in our own way. I was left with restless holes in my heart and head. Each filled with whys. My hope was that time would fill the holes with happy memories spent with a big brother who died living his dream. He joined the Kiyagamohag (Meskwaki’s Warrior Society) at the earliest possible age (18 winters).Our Meskwakis were known as intense warriors who showed little mercy to their enemies.

Another significant reason was Elyshia. Her family moved to a Sauk village near the Rock River three full moons ago. Her ailing grandmother needed their support. Heightened concern about safety in a Meskwaki village on the Kickapoo River probably was a factor in their decision to move. Elyshia was unhappy about leaving. I promised to see her soon and

Rock River was our first destination. Chaska also was anxious to spend time with Elyshia's sister, Chepi.

I wanted to canoe the Mississippi River for adventures and learning experiences. My family supported the trip for these reasons and thought the timing was right. Some of their concerns eased when they learned Chaska and Keme had joined the adventure.

Uncle Leno advised: Danger exists in many places for a Meskwaki. With their allies, weapons, treachery, and appetite for our land and resources, Frenchmen appear to control our destiny. Fortunately, now we have a shaky truce with the French. They and their tribal allies are located along the Mississippi River to the Great Sea. Don't let that ruin the adventure. In your favor, the land and Mississippi River are so large that most is free from tight French control. Chaska's command of Sioux, French, and Algonquian tongues will be very helpful;

While canoeing, you will be like sitting ducks. Be alert, be fearful, but don't close your eyes or senses to the wonders and good people you will meet;

The Mississippi River grows into a giant of giants as it continues south, drinking other rivers and streams. You'll be surprised at the large waves and rough water you encounter with bad weather and windy conditions. Our light canoes with round bottoms act like sails against winds, especially crosswinds. All of you are expert paddlers, be smart and trust your skills;

Don't canoe on the Mississippi at night. It's risky because you can't see clearly. Swamping a canoe in the dark could be a disaster. *F*og is worse than darkness because it's unpredictable. ***Stay off the river when it's foggy enough to reduce visibility less than a mile, and always have a plan where to meet if you are separated unexpectedly.***

We were within sight of the Wisconsin River. Yesterday, the sun was high in the sky when we left the village. We spent the earlier part of the day packing canoes and saying goodbye. When we approached the Wisconsin, we decided to spend one more night on 'our Kickapoo' and get an early start to greet the Mississippi River.

Last night, a beautiful strawberry moon lit the sky. It would be easy to remember our departure date. Chaska announced, "I am going to take a little Kickapoo sand and throw it, untouched by other waters, directly into the Great Sea." While Keme and I were still thinking what a dumb yet unique idea, Chaska removed a mussel shell from his medicine pouch and packed it full of Kickapoo sand.

Too excited to think about eating, we shoved our canoes into the Kickapoo. We had no idea whether we would paddle our canoes back or walk. Such a small detail didn't matter. Uncle Leno told us that the journey down the Mississippi River to the Great Sea and back was only about 4,000 miles.

First Day

Hello Wisconsin River! Hello Mississippi River! Look out from the Kickapoo River, here come three brave paddlers!

Within minutes, we entered the Wisconsin, which flows into the Mississippi from a relatively level river bed that spreads and slows the Wisconsin's merging speed. It also causes the Wisconsin to splinter and create mudflats and messy side pools of water, and small islands that vary in size, depending on how much rain had fallen upstream.

On a high, I paddled like we were in a mad dash to make the Great Sea by sunset. The river's current, plus our vigorous paddling, gobbled up the distance. We covered the 20 plus miles in a couple of hours, and could see the Mississippi River. Since I had been downstream several times with Uncle Leno to gather river cane, I was leading the way for the first day.

After today, Keme would be the lead canoe, Chaska would be next, and I would bring up the rear. Keme could see, hear, smell, read currents, and nearby woods far better than Chaska or Tyr. We wanted to protect our brains that's why Chaska was in the middle.

We had all canoed on the Mississippi a number of times, mostly upstream to Prairie du Chien, La Crosse, and points farther north. It wasn't a stretch to claim that all of us were expert canoe paddlers and swimmers, and we had participated in these activities hundreds of times in all sorts of streams, lakes, and conditions.

Beaching my canoe onto the Wisconsin's northern bank, Chaska and Keme joined me. They wanted to know why we were racing. I answered, "This was a warm-up for the days to come!" Hungry and happy, it was time for food. We shared the meal from a 400 foot high bluff on the Mississippi River's west bank, where there was a panoramic view of our homeland. Here, we could see the Mississippi River was about the same width as the Wisconsin; both had a greenish tinge, with the Mississippi River slightly greener. The large island facing Prairie du Chien was visible, as were the village and corn fields next to Prairie du Chien. The backdrop in most directions was more tree-topped bluffs. We knew the layout of the surrounding land, and while we couldn't see our village, we could point out the line-of-sight direction and wave goodbye to our home on the Kickapoo.

Downriver, we saw more high bluffs on both sides. The cane field was more than 30 miles away, so we could only spend a little time sightseeing and be there before dark. Near the cane field was a Meskwaki village where we spent the night. It was less than half the size of our village, and I had been there with Uncle Leno. We were welcomed with open arms, enjoyed a tasty evening meal, and joined a fire circle, where we shared our Mississippi adventure plan. These folks knew our elders and treated us like we were important. They wished us well on our journey. Then insisted we sleep in their lodges and provided a delicious send-off breakfast.

Rock River, where it joined the Mississippi River, was Elyshia's village's location and our next major destination. It was about 100 miles downriver. Uncle Leno told us, "A 13-mile stretch of big rapids will introduce the Rock River."

Strange Fireflies

We planned to reach the rapids and Rock River within the next few days. The scenery was almost identical to our first day. High bluffs were on both sides of the river with sand or gravel beaches. Emotions settled down from novice highs, and we began coasting close together and talking about the beautiful wildlife, and scenery on both sides of the river. Realizing our speed had slowed, we compensated by paddling hard until sundown.

Tired, we pulled our canoes onto a sandy river bank. A few fireflies were blinking tiny lights. Usually, they start flashing before dark and continue blinking for a while. We made our campfire and ate food provided by our new Meskwaki friends. As darkness deepened, we stopped adding wood to the campfire. Keme alerted us to flashing lights across the river.

As we watched, the intensity of the lights increased, and the flashing became more synchronized. The light show had our undivided attention. Chaska timed the flashing. The bright flashes took about three counts, and the darkness between flashes lasted about nine counts. The blinking lights just kept on blinking. To us, this was a mystery.

Curious and ignoring Uncle Leno's advice, we loaded into one canoe and paddled across the dark, calm river. Quietly drifting into the bank, we approached the lighted area on foot like thieves in the night. We brought axes and knives. Why? The unknown had us worried!

The bright, pulsating lights continued unabated. We found two adjacent scrub oaks housing thousands of fireflies. On close examination, they were no different from fireflies we had captured and played with when youngsters. They had the same tiny black wings, white stripes, and a luminescent waxy underbelly tip that remained lit for a while when pinched off.

Our presence didn't disturb their flashing rhythm. We yelled and struck one of the trees with an axe, and the flashing rhythm was unchanged. The mysterious blinking lights were fireflies, thousands of them huddled together in the trees, flickering together in near-perfect rhythm.

Chaska reminded us, "Your Aunt Meda warned us about deceiving eyes; this is lighting bugs doing their thing, if that's strange, so be it." We paddled back across the river.

As we prepared to bed down, Keme began talking nonstop about elders discussing tribal myths and events around fire circles. He asked, "Do you remember that witches and ghosts are evil spirits?" Not needing a response, he continued: Many of our elders believe witches are real—not myths. They are near us and we need to recognize them, and not make them angry. They travel at night and emit flashes of light from their mouths that illuminate their surroundings. By the hissing sound they make, you can hear them pass. It's impossible to kill a witch even if you shoot it in the heart. It goes home, and sometimes a person exposed to their light will drop dead. A witch's evil power is so strong it can perform a wicked act on someone far away. A witch carries a charm around about the size of your thumb. When a witch wants to harm a person, it tells its charm where to go, what person to harm, and how to hurt them. A witch can find and hurt you even if you hide inside your lodge. If I hear a hissing sound, I say we get out of here pronto!

Chaska replied, "Keme you can't believe such crap? Besides, lights were coming from their ass-holes, not their mouths."

A wound-up Keme responded, "Chaska, with those weird lights blinking across the river, for all I know, those balls of fireflies could be coming from the mouths of evil witches shaped like trees. Maybe that's two witches meeting to decide what to do with us."

I interrupted the conversation, "Keme, I need sleep. Wake me if you hear hissing. If you don't, we will see if the trees are still light-spitting witches planning to harm us in the morning ." Pulling my blanket around my head, I tried to go to sleep.

Keme's scream freaked me out."Tyr, Tyr, I hear the hissing; we've got to get out of here!" He yanked my blanket off. I jumped up and tripped over my feet. Keme's loud laugh told me that *'I had been had.'* "You rat," I yelled. "Yeah," he replied, "I wanted to test your witch ignorance and bravery. You would have run over me if you hadn't tripped." Chaska, half-asleep, realized Keme had scared me. We laughed, Keme threw another log on the fire, and we went to sleep with the lights blinking.

We were all awake before dawn, and no lights were visible. After breakfast and breaking camp, we crossed the river and examined the scrubby trees. While a few fireflies were in the trees, most had either moved on or lay dead on the ground. What caused this synchronized flashing was a mystery, at least to us. Already, we proved we had a lot to learn. I wouldn't have believed a bunch of fireflies could have frightened Keme a lot, me more than I liked, and Chaska a little too. Nevertheless, they did!

When we pushed off toward the middle of the river, Keme yelled, "Don't forget, our fire-circle witch experts said that we have three more nights before knowing we are safe from those witches."

Special Encounters

Midmorning, we pulled into a small, fast river. Fighting the upstream current, we landed our canoes on a gravel bar. Nearby, Keme found a spring squirting ice-cold water. We drank our fill and replaced the water in our storage skins. Munching on pemmican, we decided to kill game at our next campsite.

Feeling frisky after the break, we launched canoes at about the same time. Being the closest to the brush and trees on the downside of the river, I glanced back to make sure I was clear of the other canoes. Underestimating the speed and power of the river, a jagged limb ripped the trim on the left side of my canoe. Luckily it wasn't serious. Still, the damage needed repairing before the split widened.

It was early afternoon with plenty of daylight left when we landed our canoes on a thin, lengthy slice of sandy beach that was clinging to two large bluffs separated by a creek-sized stream.

Repairing the banged-up canoe was my job, while Chaska and Keme went to kill meat to last us a few days. Uncle Leno had informed us that a man would have to be a lazy lout, a poor shot or blind to go hungry on the Mississippi River this time of year. He was right. Game, big and small, especially deer, seemed to be everywhere, and the Mississippi, and feeder streams were teeming with fish. We preferred red meat. Fish was our choice only when we were lazy or had few options.

We packed plenty of birch patching strips, and pine gum resin. To do the repair work I needed fire to melt the pine resin glue, a knife, a slice of birch bark, and a little sweat. It didn't take long to collect wood for the night, start a roaring fire, and complete the trim repair. Admiring my work, I was oblivious to the outside world. Suddenly two canoes skidded onto the beach.

Two guys about my age were in a large canoe loaded with birch bark containers. An older guy steered the second canoe. It was also loaded with containers. Focused on the creek, and hoping to find a spring, and enough cold, clear water to enjoy a swim, they didn't realize anyone was on the small beach until they landed. They were Sioux. The older guy, Kola, was a friendly talker who could speak and understand a little Algonquian; enough with signing that we could communicate. They were from a village located close to the Mississippi River near Lake Superior. I told Kola that we're from near Prairie du Chien and my friends will soon return with fresh meat. There should be enough to share.

Kola responded, "Thanks, my friends are tired of paddling, and so am I. While they swim, I'll find some watercress or greens, and boil a delicious rice stew to go with your meat. It's my mother's recipe. Our containers are filled with rice."

Chaska would be delighted, and Keme would be suspicious, although okay with sharing food. I helped drag the Sioux canoes near ours and gathered more firewood while they were swimming and finding greens.

While searching for wood, I discovered a trail aimed toward the blufftop. Following the trail would have to wait. Kola returned with greens in hand. While his young friends swam, Kola filled a large pot with water, rice, greens, and spices. Soon the boiling rice was sending forth wonderful spicy scents, and we heard friendly voices headed our way. Chaska and Keme had killed a plump young deer and turkey, and already met the two young Sioux.

Immediately, Chaska and Kola became engaged in animated conversation. They both had Santee Dakota Sioux blood and Kola knew of Chaska's father and other Sioux relatives. Two complete strangers became instant friends, and we decided to spend the night together.

I climbed the bluff trail while Chaska, Keme, Kola, and his two friends finished preparing the feast. The path was easy to follow to the top where a slightly curving river could be seen for many miles. There was a group of four canoes lazily floating down the river. Much closer two canoes near the western bank were inching their way upstream.

When I returned to camp, feasting already had begun. Kola's melt-in-your-mouth rice with chopped greens, and spices was a delicious addition to the nicely browned venison and turkey. We devoured all the rice and a big part of the tender, juicy meat. No rice grew near our village, so it was a seldom served treat.

Kola and friends were delivering rice to a large Sioux village on the Iowa River. They invited our group to travel with them and promised we would be welcomed at the Sioux village. Our next stop at Rock River was about 40 miles north of the Iowa River, so we agreed to stick together until we encountered the rapids above the Rock River.

The sun was beginning to set, when I announced my plan to sleep on the blufftop for a better view of the sunset, and tomorrow's sunrise. Keme and I climbed the bluff with blankets, weapons, water, and leftovers.

There were high wispy clouds floating overhead. By the time our fire made crackling noises, directly to the west, hovering horizon to horizon over the mountain bluffs, was a thick, jagged line of smoky white clouds separated by two almost parallel paths of blue sky. We saw first the bluffs, then a small sliver of blue sky parallel to the bluffs. Next, the jagged line of clouds appeared to be pasted out of place against the higher expanse of the blue sky.

It was beautiful until the sun dropped below the jagged line of smokey white clouds; then, it became a spectacular panorama. The sun was no longer a solid golden orb. Rather, *it exploded* into three sources of light. The first light filled the sky above the jagged cloud line. It was a giant fan of yellow, gold, and muted shades of orange that kept fanning out the higher it was in the now darkened blue-layered sky. The second was a thin, segregated horizontal line of light between the cloud bottoms and the top of the bluffs. This bright yellow dissipated on both sides into light oranges having a different color of blue separating the two jagged lines. A third source was the reflection of the others on the Mississippi River. This light across the once-green river consisted of beautiful layers. First, there was a reflection of the blackened bluffs having shades of black and purple. Next there was a reflection of the sun, and it was a jagged oval orange fringed on both sides with shades of blue. Finally, the remaining blue-black river reflected muted orangish from the vast fan-shaped light from above. It almost seemed like darkness was seeping from Earth rather than descending from the sky.

Keme had little interest in sunsets. He did believe this was a complicated sunset. It consolidated the sky, clouds, bluffs, river, and reflections in one outstanding portrait, having a unique and amazing array of colors and patterns.

The next morning we awoke to a boring sunrise and made our way down the bluff, where large perch and crappie were being fried. Kola was interested in a sunset and sunrise description. My report: "The sunrise wasn't worth the climb. The sunset was spectacular. You should have seen it."

Chaska and Kola spent most of the night talking about families, hunting, and other topics. The two sleep-deprived young Sioux wished they had slept on the blufftop.

We finished our meal and were loading the canoes when Chaska asked Kola, "How are you guys prepared to defend yourselves?" Kola pulled out a musket and hatchet hidden between birchbark containers. He told us, "We each have these plus our knives and we know how to use them."

The rice canoes led the way. Staying close, we were both relaxed and excited, knowing soon we would be amongst our Sauk friends. Before midday, the rice canoes beached above the rapids just north of the Rock River. We slid in beside them and exchanged warm goodbyes, hoping we would meet again someday. Kola handed us a gift packet that contained rice and some of his mother's spices. Kola wasn't that concerned about the rapids. His only advice was, "Stay in the middle of the river."

Two special encounters: The most interesting sunset of my life, which I couldn't describe, and three new Sioux friends, whom I never met again. They were present, then, except for pleasant memories, disappeared from my life.

Uncle Leno told us, "There are lots of good people on the Mississippi River." So far that's all we had met.

Elyshia and Rock River

The big rapids matched Uncle Leno's description. Land next to the river was flatter, and the tall bluffs had given way to a few small bluffs, hills, and distant mountains. Islands with varying shapes and sizes continued to be scattered in the river, although they were absent from this stretch of rapids.

The weather was nice and sunny. We didn't ignore Kola's advice to stay in the middle of the river. Still, scouting the rapids, we found, as Uncle Leno warned, they were BIG. There was a channel in the center of the river surrounded by large rocks reaching out from both banks. The tough white-water rapids were closer to each side of the river. There was little or no wind, so it seemed we could stay in the mid-channel without much danger, even with loaded canoes. Kneeling on our knees, we lowered our centers of gravity to improve paddle control.

If anyone took on significant water, we decided all would head to the nearest bank and dump water. Shifting weights of sloshing water in an open canoe makes it easy to lose control. We underestimated the unpredictable cross currents. Once I took on too much water, requiring us to beach. Working across the rapids to the bank and back to the channel took all our rapid running skills. Keme hit a submerged rock that swung his canoe around. Before regaining control, his canoe was half-full of water, requiring another risky trip to the river bank. Chaska? He complained about us delaying his progress.

We had some control when running rapids on smaller white water rivers, even when the rivers dumped us. Canoeing around these large rocks and through big waves felt like one mistake, or a large puff of wind from the wrong direction could easily swamp or overturn our light and loaded canoes. We agreed to avoid rapids like these in windy, rainy weather. It would be safer to line or portage our canoes or wait for better weather.

As we approached the last rapid, the river significantly changed direction for the first time. Its southerly flow turned to a westerly flow then angled toward the south again. Ahead, on the left, we could see the Rock River confluence.

Past the rapids, we beached and asked an old man, sorting out nets, if he knew where Morning Bear's family lived. With little more than a glance, he replied, "Go a few miles up Rock River, and you will find his village on the south side of the river."

As directed, we found about 25 lodges overlooking the river. And soon spotted Elyshia's mother, Chloe, talking to a young guy and noticed several dogs were yapping. She greeted us and seemed pleased we were here. After introducing us to Hassun, her nephew, she told us: I need to share some sad news. My mother recently died, so we are in mourning; Also, Elyshia is confined to the menstrual lodge and can't have male company for another day or two; Morning Bear is leading a hunting party and will be gone for several more days; Chepi is here. She's already made plans to spend the next couple of nights with a friend. She will be mad if I don't let her know Chaska is here, so I'll tell her tomorrow morning; At least for the night, you can squeeze into our lodge to sleep; the mosquitoes are terrible outside. I do have a pot of stew simmering.

When Hassun learned we were going to canoe the Mississippi River until it met the Great Sea, he latched onto us like we were long-lost friends. He said, "Right now my friends are gathering at a nearby swimming hole, where we have lots of fun. If you're not too tired, let's unload your canoes and go swimming." Reading our reaction, Chloe approved, "Go have fun. The stew will still be here." We went and had a fun time!

Hassun was a friendly, well-liked athlete, and held his own with all of us. He swam like a fish, held his breath like a turtle, dived like Chaska, out-talked me, and surprised Keme with his strength.

The next day, Hassun and friends had plans to canoe rapids and challenged us to rerun the rapids we had just been through, except follow them through the tough parts. We couldn't risk damaging our canoes. They wanted to show off their expertise and volunteered to take turns with us in their canoes. We agreed, although I wouldn't participate if Elyshia was free. Chloe learned that Elyshia would have to spend another day in the menstrual lodge.

I slept in Elyshia's area of the lodge. Her collection of herbs and flowers created a pleasing odor similar to our medicine man's lodge. The area was pleasant. The image in my mind was Elyshia. Keme and Chaska stayed in Hassun's nearby lodge.

Early the next morning, four canoes, three loaded with an extra body, retraced our way to the rapids. Their canoes had special features—portable deer skin coverings were lashed to the canoe tops, which kept most splashing water from filling the canoes.

We had a fantastic time! The challenging rapids dumped each competitor at least once in the mighty Mississippi River. Counting style points, the two best rapid runners were Chaska and Hassun. While they competed for the championship, the rest of us were judges. Chaska went first, and Hassun followed. Chaska was flawless until right before the last rapid which was introduced by a huge rock. Passing the rock, Chaska did a handstand on the canoe's bottom. With his feet straight up in the air, he was successfully flushed through the monster rapid without using his paddle. Keme and I cheered, thinking Chaska had won the contest.

Hassun, following close behind, also had a flawless run. He saw Chaska's move, and he too stood on his hands and head. Adding a touch, he kicked the big rock with his right foot when he whizzed by. Somehow he maintained his and the canoe's balance, while being flushed through without using his paddle. As the two heroes made their way to the bank, the judges yelled approval. Both competitors incorporated acrobatics like, ho-hum, they were born to do it. By a kick, Hassun was the winner!

I rode down with Hassun. On the way back to the village I congratulated him for having more body control and balance running river rapids than anyone I had ever seen. Downplaying his expertise, Hassun replied, "We practice crazy stuff all the time. When I saw Chaska's flashy maneuver, I knew if I was going to win, I needed to improvise, and was lucky enough to pull it off. If it failed, I would be soaked. I am a getting-wet expert, so it was no big deal."

Hassun mentioned canoeing the Mississippi River past the Missouri River to a trading post at Kaskaskia several times, but never to the Great Sea, and asked if he could join us. "It's a long way to the Missouri River," I replied, "We could use a guide and an expert paddler. It would be terrific if you traveled with us. I do need approvals from Keme and Chaska." Immediately after learning about the request, Keme and Chaska agreed that Hassun would be an excellent addition to our group. Hassun's mother talked to each of us and gave her blessing. His father was dead. So it was settled, Hassun was the new adventurer on our Mississippi River adventure team.

Hassun and Keme coordinated the details required to seam our team together. Chaska spent most of his time for the next two days with Chepi, and I spent mine with Elyshia.

When Elyshia was released from the menstrual lodge, I was waiting with a large grin and quickened pulse. I wanted to put my arms around her, but that would display too much public affection. Reaching for her hand, I squeezed it hard. In return, she squeezed my hand as hard as she could, confirming what we both wanted to know. We hurried to her lodge, where Chloe and Elyshia's Aunt Kanti were waiting. Elyshia announced that she wanted to collect healing herbs on the island across the river, introduce me to the medicine man, and talk about many things. Chloe said that was fine, although Elyshia needed to be home by dark. Elyshia, a focused bundle of energy, declared, "We will have a picnic on the island where we will pick strawberries. I'll pack something to eat, and find a couple of baskets while Tyr gets his canoe ready to cross the river."

In the canoe, we giggled like the teenagers we were. Elyshia was excited and bubbling over to talk about her triple goals to become a herbalist, healer, and medicine woman. She was equally excited to hear news about my activities, including the Mississippi River adventure.

The island was a flat-topped, elongated small mountain covered with rich soil and scattered woodlands. Elyshia had spent considerable time here with her aunt searching for medicinal plants to help heal sick villagers. I paddled upriver until she told me, "Pull in here and you will see a wonderful spot with beautiful scenery and strawberry fields."

It was close to perfect. Nature had whittled a place where in the distance, one could see the Rock River and the Mississippi River, both upstream and downstream of the Rock River confluence. Also, it was an elevated, smooth area where we could see several wild strawberry patches, flowers, and scattered fields of young corn, and vegetables guarded by the forest. Unknown to us at the time, this close-to-perfect island later became the location of famous Rock River Villages.

Elyshia pointed at a grassy sheltered spot where we spread our blanket. Lying down, we forgot the activities Elyshia had outlined to her mother. Passionately we began touching, kissing, and pressing willing bodies together as we explored the path of sexual desires to oneness.

Clinging together gleams gone from eyes, two contented lovers lost track of time. The sun finally warned us if we wanted strawberries, we'd better start picking. We freshened up at a nearby spring, ate a little food, and each with a basket entered the closest strawberry patch. It was loaded with plump, ripe berries. We ate some while we quickly filled the baskets. They were delicious. ***Life was more delicious!***

Enough daylight remained to meet Chloe's curfew. Victoriously, with our strawberry haul in hand, we arrived at the lodge just before dark. As warned, the mosquitoes were terrible. They quickly forced us into the lodge. Again, I slept near Elyshia's collection of herbs. It was close enough to her bed that we held hands, and just touching her was a thrill. Fulfilled and tired, sleep soon found us.

Chloe prepared a delicious breakfast of corn cakes smeared with maple syrup and bear fat, along with fresh strawberries, and tender, juicy beaver livers. She asked Elyshia about today's activities. Elyshia's plan was ready: "If it's okay with Tyr, I would like to introduce him to our medicine man early this morning. Then, if he needs to make final arrangements with the guys about leaving tomorrow, he can take care of that. Later, if we have time, we could spend it on the island exploring the eastern edge and picking more strawberries."

The village medicine man was outside his lodge and seemed pleased that Elyshia cared enough to introduce us. He had kind words and great expectations for Elyshia's future as a healer. He reported, "Elyshia already knows more about healing herbs than anyone in the village and has helped deliver two babies."

Keme and Chaska were at Hassun's lodge, handling and admiring his late-model French musket. The only change to our plans was the addition of Hassun, his canoe, and belongings. My assignment was to meet them on the river below Morning Bear's lodge at sunrise tomorrow, ready to travel.

Elyshia and I paddled up Rock River toward another island rendezvous. Now we were facing each other and not giggling. She confided, "I have a new feeling of calmness and love. I thought I loved you, now, I can't imagine living without you." I assured her that I had been in love with her since our first awkward meeting on the Kickapoo.

We climbed the same rocky trail, and I followed Elyshia to a distant grassy spot, near a huge oak tree, where we spread our blanket. I laid down ready to trade sweet nothings. Elyshia pointed to a large oak tree and whispered, "Just be quiet for a little while, and you will see something extra special." It was several families of precious bluebirds. Soon, they began darting to the ground, picking up worms, and insects to feed their nestlings. Passion gave way to watching the wonder of these beautiful, caring parents taking care of their babies.

Holding each other, passion soon regained control. It was a softer, quieter passion. We knew our destination, although the sensuous unleashing of sexual desire, lust, and fulfillment never follows an identical path, especially in the presence of precious bluebirds. Still, we found the way.

Two lovers had plenty of time to talk. In a couple of weeks, Elyshia had planned to try making contact with the spirit world. Her medicine man would provide instructions, and powders similar to my vision quest experiences. This was part of the path to becoming a medicine woman. She wanted to know about my experiences. I told her that my spiritual guide was a blue-eyed black panther and my quest was filled with weird dreams or hallucinations, brought on by consuming mind-twisting powder provided by the medicine man. She wanted to know more about Aunt Meda and whether she was a medicine woman.

Aunt Meda had considerable knowledge about herbal remedies and healing. Her version of magic showed how people could be fooled by what appeared to be magic.Therefore, I didn't believe she was a medicine woman.

From my medicine pouch, I removed Aunt Meda's old guilder coin and the two small black stones found during my vision quest, and put them in Elyshia's hand. Choking back tears, she held them close to her heart and said that she could feel the energy in all three and would keep the treasures until I returned.

We discussed our futures. Because of the wars and chaos, we couldn't do much planning. Whatever the future brought, we wanted to face it together. When I returned from the Mississippi River adventure, we would be married.

Again, we were back at Elyshia's lodge before dark. Being polite, no one mentioned strawberries we didn't have. The night was a blur. I remember waking up and hugging Elyshia, who placed a basket filled with healing herbs, powders, and salves, in my hands. She quickly described when and how to use them.

As the last in our small canoe flotilla, I waved goodbye to Elyshia and family. We covered the short distance to the Mississippi River, where I relaxed, knowing Hassun was leading us.

Elyshia, was in my mind and heart. As Anna would sometimes say, "You have it bad!" Luckily, for a little while, all I had to worry about was *keeping up with Chaska's canoe.*

Flint River Warriors

Our next significant destination was the Missouri River confluence with the Mississippi River. With the morning sun shining on our backs, we mainly traveled west rather than south, dodging the islands that choked the river. Hassun was leading at a rapid pace, and it was an effort to keep up. Being the last canoe weaving around view-blocking islands, I seldom saw Hassun during the first 20 miles, my eyes were on Chaska.

After more than two hours of this tiring routine, Hassun, followed by Keme and Chaska, landed on a small sandy strip. We hadn't eaten. Chloe, Aunt Kanti, Elyshia, and Chepi had packed an excellent meal that quickly disappeared.

Hassun informed us that from Rock River to the Missouri River is about 300 miles of sparsely populated countryside. In the first 100 miles there are a few scattered Mascouten villages and hunting camps. Farther south toward the Missouri River, there are Illini and their brother tribes—Cahokia and Kaskaskia. If we stay close to the Mississippi River, there isn't much danger unless the Illini or Sioux are on the warpath. In about 10 days, we should see the Missouri River. Lousy weather, repairs, or confrontations can cause delays.

"Tomorrow, near the flint hills and a friendly Mascouten village, we will dig awhile for high-grade flint. It's an experience worth a little time."

Early the next morning, three canoes followed Hassun several miles west up a winding Flint River. Flatland stretched between the river and bluffs on the south side. The tall limestone bluffs watched over streams, hills, and valleys like mothers guarding their children. Hassun turned up a creek, flowing from the bluffs' direction.

The impressive Mascouten village was enclosed by vertical posts about 12 feet high. It sat on the top of a leveled hill, about 15 feet above creek level. Landing our canoes, several villagers greeted us. Hassun, full of surprises, began speaking their language like a long-lost relative. He informed us that his mother was half Mascouten and his uncle, Big Bear, was a war chief for the village.

Feeling like special guests, we entered the fortification through an open gate and were welcomed by an unsightly mixture of jammed lodges, tipis, and clutter. The tidy and impressive fortress walls were misleading. Amongst the mess, groups of people were working and playing. Hassun led us directly to Big Bear's tipi.

Big Bear wasn't available. His eldest son, Kitchi, using the Sauk tongue, welcomed us and told Hassun that he, Kitchi, had bad news. An Illini hunting party is planning to attack our village, and our council is now deciding on defensive actions. Hassun replied, "We were passing by and just wanted to say hello and find a few flint nodules." Kitchi advised, "I recommend you stay with us here in the fortified area until we know the council's decision. The Illini devils are a couple of miles downstream on the big river, getting high and would kill you for laughs. *Tomorrow we may be fighting for our lives."* We made clear we would stay and help in anyway we could.

After a brief wait, Big Bear assembled every male that could fight, including us. His words were in Mascouten. I understood there was a path in the forest needing protection and little else. When the meeting closed, Kitchi provided us with a short translation: Big Bear believes the attack will start near dawn tomorrow, so we have to be ready; Our spy estimates there are about 40 Illini warriors; We have two hunting parties out, leaving only sixteen warriors in the fort; Unknown to the Illini, we have extra muskets and plenty of lead and powder; Our warriors have practiced battle positions, so they know their firing ports; The devils may launch fire arrows. If they do, it will be at their peril because their launching distance is within the range of our sharpshooters; They may send a few sharpshooters down the steep, narrow, seldom-used mountain pathway on the south side of our fort. Both sides of the path are covered with trees, sticky brambles, and bushes that need an axe to penetrate. So Big Bear is working on a plan to counter that possibility. I will assign you guys jobs to help inside the fort.

Without hesitation, my big mouth informed Kitchi: With the agreement of my friends, you can have all your warriors protecting the village. You know Hassun. The rest of us are Meskwakis from the Prairie du Chien area. I am Tyr. Our people hate the Illini; We are young experts with our weapons. Like silent panthers, we can be killers in the woods. Keme has already killed an Iroquois warrior and can track others or lose himself in the woods quicker and quieter than anybody in this fort; I am, perhaps, the best atlatl slinger along the Mississippi River. Chaska is also an outstanding atlatl slinger; We would be proud to show our skills and plant some spears and arrows in the devils. The three of us have spent our lives in the woods together. Hassun, as you know, is an expert with his musket. ***It's almost like Wisaka sent us here on purpose to help in the woods and not here in the fort;***

If someone could lead us up the trail, we can find the best ambush positions and become one with the forest. If the devils have to travel single file and start traveling down the mountain before daylight, we can ambush them; The earlier they start in the morning, the better our chance will be to stop them. All four of us stood and locked arms. Kitchi's answer was, "Come with me!" He took us to Big Bear, where my remarks were repeated.

Big Bear growled in Sauk, "I know Hassun, the rest of you get your *silent* weapons, and let's see what you can do." When we returned with our weapons, a man-sized target was waiting. Two leaders were with Big Bear. The other warriors and helpers were already preparing to defend the fort. I had six spears. Big Bear paced about 40 feet away from the target, dropped a marker, and pointed at me, ordering, "You're first, stand here!" Then he paced off another 20 feet, dropped another marker and ordered, "When I yell 'NOW!' as quick as you can, sling three spears from each launching location."

Slinging spears as fast as possible was a favorite competitive game between myself and Chaska. I placed all six spears on the ground, pointing at the target. Then, I held up a hand, took a couple of practice atlatl turns, leaned over and picked up a spear, and heard "NOW!" Thud, Thud, Thud, three spears landed close to the target's center (the last two very close). From the 60 foot launch location, three more spears hit the target. These, on average, were about an inch below the first volley.

All of Chaska's spears hit the target and Keme had his arrows flying on target and threw his tomahawk 40 feet into the target's center.

Big Bear huddled with his leaders. After a few minutes, he reported they were impressed with our skills and thought the plan could work, although very concerned with our youth and the consequences of sending us into battle if we were killed. I told Big Bear, "We are older than we look and have completed our Vision Quests. We sat around many fire circles, listening to stories about French treachery with Illini and other tribes torturing and killing almost 1,000 Meskwakis and Mascoutens at Fort Pontchartrain. My brother, Mingan, was among those killed. Our group wants to *do what's right,* and that's helping protect your fort by blocking the mountain trail."

The decision was '**GO**.' Kitchi would be the lone warrior and leader of our group. They assigned Taregan as scout, he was an old guy, who knew the trail like the back of his hands. Taregan, Kitchi, and Hassun had muskets, while we three Meskwakis had our silent weapons. Within two hours, our team was outfitted and following Taregan up and down the mountain trail, determining ambush locations and who would man each.

There were only a few places on the steep, narrow trail where two warriors could stand side-by-side. The path had several sharp turns and was so narrow and overgrown that only a group leader or the last in line could directly shoot at adversaries. If spread out, they still would be easy pickings. There was one short and dead-end side trail.

We set ambush locations on the lower half of the trail where we could trap the devils. By dark, our ambush positions and signals were planned. Keme would be the first to strike, waiting until the last devil passed before striking from the rear. The rest of us were strung out down the trail on alternating opposite sides. The highest to lowest on the trail after Keme were Tyr, Chaska, Hassun, Taregan and Kitchi. Kitchi was in sight of the fort, so he could warn them if our mission failed. There were two extremely sharp turns in our killing stretch. The first turn was just below Keme's strike point.

After a long night manning positions and chewing pemmican, a chilly, hazy, darkened dawn came creeping in from the sky. During the night, we heard a panther screaming, which I took as an excellent omen—my spiritual soulmate was near.

Keme and I heard the devils creeping down the mountain first. They were traveling in pairs of two. I counted six before Keme killed the last pair of devils, so quick and quiet (helped by the isolating sharp turn) those in front never knew it happened.

Stepping in the back of the new last-in-line, it took several quick steps before I planted a spear in his back. The commotion alerted the next devil, and he turned and lifted his musket. Before he could fire, he was downed by a second spear. Shooting warriors in the back or by surprise was not heroic. Village safety was our duty. We were lucky. Killing four devils was easier than killing confused buffaloes.

When and if Keme and I cleared the rear, we were to start yelling Meskwaki war whoops, so the rest of the team would start picking off the remaining devils. We were loud yellers!

Chaska killed another devil. This one fired at him, and the shooting began. Our ambushes, helped by the terrain, worked until one devil was left. He kept running down the trail toward the village, and Kitchi shot him.

We reported to Kitchi, who was amazed to hear eight devils were dead and none of us were seriously hurt. Aside from some scratches and bruises, none of us were really injured. The only exception was Keme, who somehow had raked a sharply pointed branch against the side of his forehead. Pressure from hand-held leaves was the only thing stopping the bleeding. **Wisaka had held us safely in his hands.**

From his position, Kitchi had observed the battle scene below and reported, "No serious threat to the fort occurred. The devils set fire to a tipi and made an aborted run at the fort. Now there are just a few random musket shots. The storm clouds probably ended their poorly planned suicides."

The rest of us had been oblivious to storm clouds; our focus had been on killing or being killed. Kitchi ordered, "Tyr you and Chaska follow me. I need to verify there are eight dead devils. Taregan, you and Hassan lead Keme to the fort and have the medicine man stop his bleeding."

Completing our assignment, we found all the bodies. One was barely alive. Kitchi shot him in the temple to end his misery, splattering skin, blood, brains, and bone. I had no more feelings of remorse or sympathy than I would have if it had been a wolf that attacked us. There had been so much bad blood between Meskwaki and Illini tribes that we considered each other devils worse than wild animals.

Farther up the mountain and standing over the first warrior I killed, Kitchi wondered why we didn't take scalps. We were inexperienced and too busy to think about scalping. Plus, knowing how we killed them, I wasn't proud enough to take scalps. Still mourning for my big brother, I *was proud* I upheld Meskwaki tribe's honor and killed this devil. Also, like killing my first elk, I was *proud* that I could sling my spears under pressure. *I was now a hunter and a defense warrior!* The dead warriors had feathers, and I took one from each of the two I killed. My biggest concern was salvaging spears.

Chaska asked, "Can we have their weapons?" Kitchi answered, "The possessions of any enemy killed belong to the warrior who killed them. I will help you carry your bounty to the village." Since we were farthest up the mountain, I retrieved weapons and feathers from Keme's victims.

Half sliding off the bluff, we found a crazy-with-excitement group of victorious villagers. Keme's wound was dressed and not serious. Our team stayed close to Kitchi, while he reported the trail status to Chief Big Bear, who congratulated us for an excellent plan and dramatic results.

Fires were being built, and spontaneous dancing had already started. A day and night of celebrations had commenced.

Kitchi found a lodge for us. After we were situated, Chaska unpacked his drum and rattles, then he and Hassan joined a group making music for the dancers. Keme and I milled around, trying to stay out of the way.

Later, Kitchi assembled our group and reported, "The big chief will introduce our team, including you four new warriors, to the villagers." The chief asked Kitchi to describe what our team had accomplished. Kitchi's description didn't mention the silent weapons-in-the-back part. We came away as new warriors and village celebrities.

We didn't get much sleep. Villagers (young, old, male, and female) treated us like we were special ambassadors directly anointed by *Wisaka*. At sunrise, Kitchi woke us with loud rapping and "Get Up! Our females are preparing a special meal for you heroes." With newfound energy, we thanked the Big Bear family and told them we were interested in digging a few flint nodules and would like to be on our way by midday. Kitchi replied, "Taregan will be glad to take you to the best location and teach you digging details, which will be more fun for him than helping us burn a bunch of devils. You are now village legends and welcome to stay as long as you want. If you plan to leave midday, you must start packing while I inform Taregan you need his help."

New additions to our canoes were four late-model French muskets and accessories, plus plenty of powder and lead. We were thrilled with the new possessions.

Taregan came from the fort with a sizable and reinforced birch box. Some smooth, hard rocks to use as hammers were inside. We would use the box to carry our nodules, if we found any. A flint expert, Taregan, declared: Around here, you can look in any direction and find flint. The streams contain many small, splintered pieces of flint. Near the limestone bluffs or hill sides, you can dig and find chunks of flint bound together with limestone, and other rocks; Good-sized nodules are desirable, because a proficient Flintknapper can get more spear points, plus pieces of flint used with steel strikers to start fires and fire muskets; Recognizing and digging high-grade nodules takes experience, luck, a lot of dirt/rock digging, and rock hammering.

Our time in the digging area was brief. Taregan did teach us a few things. For example, limestone containing flint usually has a darker shade and the flint will likely appear dark gray or black, and sometimes will appear glossy. Using a hammer stone, you can break a piece off a suspect rock. Then you can strike an edge against a metal striker, and sparks will show if the rock contains flint. We dug out a few good nodules.

The time spent on our knees examining rock formations, hammering specimens, digging, and finding a few nodules was enough to make us appreciate how much knowledge and work it takes to furnish flint to flintknappers, like my Uncle Chogan. However, no one from our team had any inclination to be a flint digger. We were happy being hunters and *warriors*.

Returning to the village, out of the blue, Taregan asked, "How much pine gum do you have? I want to check it." We took him to our canoes to show him, and he said, "That's not nearly enough to last you on the lower Mississippi. I've made the trip several times, and you need to double that amount. And I have plenty." It took a while to finish loading our canoes, including the gift of pine gum from Taregan. We participated in a special send-off with more than 50 new friends. One sweet, pretty young lady, named Hurit, and Hassan had a special, holding and hugging goodbye. We discovered the real reason Hassan wanted to stop here.

Then, it was down the creek, down the Flint River and down the Mississippi River toward our next destination.

Loud Weapons, Strange Rapids, and Rain

Plenty of daylight remained. We were anxious to try our new muskets, so we decided to stop above a long stretch of rapids, and challenge the rapids tomorrow.

In our Meskwaki village, there were several old Dutch and French muskets. They often misfired, were difficult to load with gunpowder and lead, and took too much time to reload and fire. The three of us had experience shooting these old weapons. We were confident our silent weapons were superior, especially when hunting because the noise from a first shot or misfire could spook an entire herd.

Hassan, the expert, volunteered to show us the advantages of our new muskets. We were all in, and after making camp, Hassan pointed to a clearing and said, "Take your silent weapons. We will have a competition to show you the musket's advantages." Hassan set up a circular-shaped target about three feet in diameter and placed it approximately 150 feet away. We each fired one practice shot. Then we lined up and simultaneously fired three shots at the target. Keme used his bow and arrows. Chaska and I used atlatls, and Hassan fired his musket. During the initial practice shots, no arrow or spear found the target. Hassan hit it. The final scores: Hassan hit the target all four times (a couple close to center), Keme and I hit it twice (none close to center), and Chaska hit it once (close to center).

Hassan was fast at reloading and aiming his musket, but took twice as long to fire his three shots as Keme, who was first to unleash all his arrows. Chaska and I tied for second place with the speed of our delivery.

Summarizing, Hassan said, "Your silent weapons are great at short distances. However, these recently built muskets can kill at greater distances. I believed 150 feet was outside your range, and I could have killed you all from that distance. Even at 150 feet, you are *amazing* with your silent weapons, and I probably would have been hit before firing my third shot. The demonstration did show at greater distances muskets like these are more accurate and have more killing power than your silent weapons. Therefore, it's important to learn how to use them. If you want, I'll teach you to become *amazing* musket experts like my father taught me." We convinced Hassan that we were eager to learn from him.

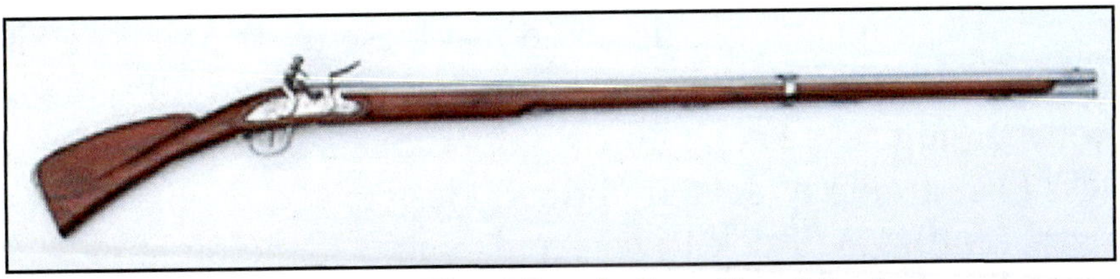

A 1717 French Flint Muzzle Loading Musket
Courtesy Charlesville Arsenal, Missouri History Museum

First, Hassan gave us a simplified description of the operation showing the cocking hammer above the trigger, which holds a piece of flint. When the trigger is pulled, the flint strikes a metal frizzen attached to a flash pan containing black gunpowder. The contact between flint and frizzen produces a shower of sparks that ignites the flash pan powder, and the flash passes through a small hole in the barrel called a touch hole. This leads to the combustion chamber, which ignites the main powder charge, and the musket discharges. The musket is loaded from the muzzle end with black powder, a lead shot, usually a round lead ball, which is pushed down the barrel with a ramrod stored underneath the barrel.

Next, following Hassan's lead, we touched and pronounced each part of our French flintlock muskets back to front, then front to back, several times. We closed our eyes and repeated the touch-and-tell maneuvers until we each got it right.

Now hungry and bushed, food, and sleep were more important than firing muskets.

Due west there were distant layers of darkened clouds headed our way. Hassan observed the clouds and noted, "We are about an hour away from the rapids, and there's no way to get through them tonight. A short distance past the rapids there's a large feeder stream we call the Hermit River. Located upstream and close by is a deserted village with old lodges now used by hunting parties. We can use it to wait out the storm." We decided this would be our next destination.

Hassan had been up and down these challenging rapids twice. He advised, "The rapids dominate an eleven-mile stretch between high limestone bluffs. Along this stretch, the river is less than a mile wide and normally less than a couple of feet deep. Unlike the Rock River rapids, there are no big rapids or channels. These rapids span the full width of the now relatively shallow river, with hundreds of dangerous, sharp rocks jutting through the surface of the river bottom. It's impassable for large, heavy boats. For our canoes, it's deep enough, and there's enough space to dodge the sharp rocks. If a canoe hits one of those sharp rocks, it could rip a hole large enough to sink the canoe."

At daybreak, there was a brisk western breeze, and layers of ominous black clouds now blotted out the western horizon. Wasting no time, we packed, jumped in our canoes, and paddled like frightened warriors. Stopping at the head of the rapids, Hassan's accurate description was confirmed. We only had to be careful and steer our canoes. Being cautious, excellent paddlers, none of our canoes were scratched by sharp rocks.

By midmorning, we turned west up the fast, slightly muddied Hermit River and after paddling several miles pulled our canoes onto a gravel bar facing the deserted village. To our surprise, it wasn't deserted. A hunting party was there. Smoke from their fire was curling upward and tossed slightly from swirling winds. We couldn't see the village as it was perched away from the river on ground elevated about 30 feet.

Two guys near our ages were messing with a canoe. They were friendly Sioux. Chaska's ability to speak the Sioux language once again helped our small group. He asked, "Could we use a couple of the lodges to wait out the coming rain?" They didn't think it was a problem. The oldest did say that Wicaka, their leader, needed to approve. They picked up their canoe, and we followed them to the village.

Despite the language barrier, we managed with Chaska interpreting, translating, and signing. Wicaka's hunting party was from the Sioux village close to the Iowa River where our recent rice-delivery friends were headed. Unbelievably, Wicaka had been at Prairie du Chien when I was an atlatl slinging kid. He met my father and laughingly recalled, "I will never forget Achak's quick takedown of the big-mouth Frenchman."

Wicaka did more than share the village, he helped protect us from the pending storm. Only eight were in his small hunting party—the two youngsters (his sons) and, counting himself, six seasoned, strong hunters. They were all safely battened down. Wicaka ordered his guys to help get our canoes and equipment into the closest, safest lodges. One of his men seemed grouchy and irritated by our presence. He did help us.

Our new saviors promptly had our four loaded canoes setting beside two lodges, and they helped unload the contents and lash canoes, bottom sides up, to the lodges. Keme and I shared a lodge; Chaska and Hassan shared the other. Hunters had kept these lodges in better condition than some of the lodges in the Mascouten village where we became warriors.

The lodge where Wicaka slept with his two boys was the largest (about 40 feet long). Here, we attended a meeting with Wicaka and his hunters. Their leader acknowledged our presence and noted, "So far we haven't felt a drop of rain. Nevertheless, a monster rainstorm is nearly on top of us. From the huge warning clouds and watching the river rise several feet, we can smell, taste, and feel the storm. Before it hits, we could use more meat and firewood." He assigned (after asking about our preferences) two Meskwakis (Keme and Hassan) to the hunting team and two (Chaska and Tyr) to the firewood team.

Wicaka and one son stayed in the village to help process meat, and store wood while maintaining a central warning base. Two of his seasoned hunters along with Keme and Hassan became the hunting team. The rest of us were split into three-man wood-gathering teams.

Chaska and I were assigned to a team led by the grouchy guy. He ordered, "Grab your hatchets and follow me!" Chaska translated his orders for me. Following directions, we stuck to him like leeches. Within a quarter of a mile, an area of downed trees and saplings appeared. Chaska and I weren't afraid of hard work and had gathered lots of firewood. We quickly hacked, untangled and pulled big arm fulls of limbs. Soon we were ready to deliver the wood. The grouchy guy, Tika, tried to outrun and outwork us. After four round trips and few words, Tika told Chaska, "*Friends*, I'm worn out; you guys are excellent workers." We were pleased to be Tikas' new friends.

The hunters brought plenty of red meat while the firewood teams gathered ample wood. Wicaka was satisfied.

For awhile, there was no rain. Soon, thick, dark-gray cloud layers covered the entire sky. Below those clouds was a layer of broken, ragged clouds and a steady, relentless downpour began. We ran to our respective lodges for cover.

My 'Storm from Hell' experience had me worried about this Monster. Unlike Kickapoo River storms I had seen, this storm had no lightning, thunder or vicious winds. The massive dark clouds lingered above us for three more days and nights, hiding sun and stars and raining. The rain amount was intermittent, ranging between light and heavy showers. A light wind sporadically moved a little rain. Most of the rain fell nearly straight down to Earth. While this kind of rain and atmosphere was great for crops, it could drive a person crazy.

Our shelter was decent. There were leaks, and we needed to go outside to complete Nature's business. We couldn't dry any wet things out until the storm passed. So, for several days, we alternated between damp and soaking wet. We were in a state of wet-cold misery and lit a fire. Soon smoke told us what a bad idea that was. Unhappy sounds added to the misery. The Hermit River was flooding and making roaring noises. At the same time rain sounds had no consistent rhythm. They varied between pitter-patters, sounds of a flock of woodpeckers rapidly pecking, or raging torrents.

It was wonderful to wake up to sunshine and no rain, while witnessing the extent of the flooding was shocking. On the opposite side of the river, was an eight-foot bank protecting the beautifully wooded, hilly, and flatland from floods. Now it was a vast muddy lake. On our side of the river, the banks varied between 10 and 12 feet, and we could see water marks almost 10 feet high. We were trapped until the flooding river subsided enough for us to canoe safely.

We spent the first day of sunshine spreading and drying our possessions. The second day was like a holiday, except we watched and listened to flood waters seeking the lowest ground. We had time to relax, play competitive games, enjoy minor feasts and tease each other. The Sioux, who had no muskets, saw all our weapons, and thought we were trying to start a war. Chaska explained how we came to own muskets, and each of the eight Sioux, under Hassan's guidance, fired a musket at least twice. Keme, Chaska, and I also fired our muskets a few times.

Hassan wanted to present a gift of his second French musket, support supplies, and plenty of ammunition to Wicaka as a token of our appreciation for the aid and support of everyone in his hunting party, and we agreed. Chaska asked Wicaka for time to give a little speech and presentation to his group. All gathered near Wicaka's lodge. With lots of animation and words, Chaska thanked the Sioux and told Hassan when it was time to present our gift. Keme, Hassan, and I didn't understand what Chaska said, or Wicaka's response. We simply smiled and watched the Sioux's faces light up when Hassan delivered the gifts.

Finally, the muddy Hermit River was contained in its banks, and with the help of our Sioux friends, we launched our canoes. It felt like we flew to the Mississippi River. We spent six days and five nights with some great guys, sharing food, work, fellowship, rain, flooding, misery, drying out, relief, and Wicaka's wise and friendly leadership.

Twin Monsters (Piasa)

It's exciting when large rivers merge with the Mississippi River. At these confluences, the rivers hit each other with glancing blows whose forces create unpredictable jumbles of circulating cross currents. These conditions widely vary with the angle of contact and because of weather and other natural influences that happen upstream. Canoeing through or around these currents can be dangerous. It isn't a serious challenge for seasoned canoeists, although it can be a special high. The colors of large merging rivers help show where most of the cross-currents exist. It can take miles after the confluence before two rivers become a unified color.

We believed the Hermit River mud would affect the Mississippi River, and it did. At the confluence, there was a slightly bumpy ride, and a prominent muddy strip ran along the western bank for several miles. Then, the Mississippi River resumed its murky green color.

After a couple of pleasant, uneventful days, we spent the night less than 10 miles from the Illinois River. Hassun advised, "With an early start, we should see the Illinois River. We will be alerted to its presence when the Mississippi River makes an unusual loop from south to north. Since the Piasas, Missouri River, and Cahokia Mounds are close; we can see all of them tomorrow." All of us had heard of the Piasas. None of us Meskwakis realized we were going to stop and look closely at it. Hassun said, "You can't pass these 'monsters' on the bluff without a closer look."

On the river at daybreak, our canoes soon made the south to north change in direction. The land hid the Illinois from sight until it joined the Mississippi. Both rivers were now one and headed in an easterly direction. Along the north bank was a 20 mile stretch of about 60 foot vertical limestone bluffs topped with 20 feet of sandstone layers. Where this stretch ended and approximately 80 feet above river level, *two scary monsters* faced each other. Their age or purpose was unknown.

Chaska and I decided to climb the bluff for a closer look, and Keme wanted nothing to do with the monsters. Hassun had seen them twice before and wasn't interested in bluff climbing, so they stayed with the canoes.

The monsters' outlines had been etched into the gray sandstone, then covered with red, black, and green colors. Time, weather, and pitting from arrow, spear, and gunshot strikes had ruined the colors. While dim and ragged, the colors were still visible. The monsters were slightly different, each about the size of a large deer. They were monsters like our maneto—a ferocious underwater panther. We were on the land of the Illini, Cahokia and Kaskaskia tribes who called it Piasa. In our language, Piasa means a creature like a water panther.

It was difficult to believe anyone could have created this giant masterpiece, especially on the sheer face of a bluff 80 feet from the river level. An ancient and unknown artist had combined descriptions of different tribes' monsters, whether on land, water, or air into one composite. Then closely duplicated it with a facing image. The result was hideous enough to strike fear and fill any viewer with wonder and admiration.

Each image had four legs, eagle-shaped talons, wings of a giant bird, antlers like a deer, and a large body covered with scales. Their faces were like a man with red eyes and a beard. Each had a long tail wound around the body, over the head, back between the legs, and ending with a fish's tail.

After Chaska and I made our way back to the river bank, Keme wanted to hit the Piasas and their evil spirits with arrows. He hit the left monster on his first shot and the right monster on his second attempt. Satisfied, Keme and the rest of us headed toward the confluence of the Missouri and Mississippi Rivers.

There are many legends about the Piasa. One legend repeated by the Illini claims that many moons ago, a large bird-like creature existed that could carry grown deer in its talons. It preferred human flesh and killed many people. Hundreds of warriors attempted to kill the Piasa and failed. Fear of the Piasa spread throughout the Illini tribe.

Ouatoga, a famous Illini chief, fasted in solitude and prayed to the Great Spirit to protect his people from the Piasa. In a dream, the Great Spirit advised Ouatoga to select 20 warriors, arm each with a bow and poisoned arrow, and hide them in a specific place. Another warrior was to stand in open view, posing as an unguarded victim for the Piasa. Ouatoga chose himself as the victim and saw the Piasa eyeing him from a neighboring bluff. Immediately he began chanting the death song of a warrior. The Piasa swooped down upon the chief. As the Piasa reached the chief, each arrow flew into the beast's body. The Piasa's fearful scream of death echoed up and down the river. Ouatoga was safe, and his tribe and all people were saved forever from horrible Piasa deaths.[6]

A Piasa

---

[6] Editors Note: The original carving of two Piasas has long been destroyed. However, a copy of one is carved on a nearby bluff near Alton, Illinois. Mississippi River tourists and nearby residents regularly visit it.

A few miles away, the Missouri River merged on the opposite and western side of the mighty Mississippi. The muddy Missouri was not as wide. However, it was faster, much muddier, and hit the Mississippi with tremendous force. We stayed away from the muddy side and were flushed through with no problems.

Finding a high spot on the eastern bank, we ate and absorbed the sight, sound, and feel of these two giant rivers colliding. It sent shivers down my spine. We discussed emptying one of our canoes, then taking turns paddling it upstream and returning through the roughest part so we could really taste the collision. Trouble, time, and risk made us forget the idea.

The land separating the two rivers was shaped like an arrowhead. We found this to be true with big rivers we encountered. Big rivers we saw didn't strike each other with right-angle blows. Our visit was long before St. Louis became an important town. I had no idea, that more than 70 winters later I would stay less than 10 miles from this spot.

As we prepared to leave, two naked young guys jumped in the Missouri River and swam or were hurled, then sucked into the confluence's swirling waters. They vanished underwater a few times before coming out kicking, hollering, and laughing near our perch. Next, the river rats swam the split-colored (murky green and muddy brown) Mississippi River to the opposite bank. We could do what the kids did and have fun swimming, but not today. Besides, a muddy bath wasn't appealing. It would be cleaner and safer to keep heading toward the famous Cahokia Mounds now about 20 miles downriver.

Cahokia Mounds

The Kickapoo River country, was surrounded by hundreds of mounds or knolls shaped like animals and birds. Uncle Chogan had shown our group several of these knolls and informed us, "Similar mounds are scattered in our woodlands and located up-and-down the Mississippi River. The largest single collection is the Cahokia Mounds, located close to the confluence of the Missouri and Mississippi Rivers. Ancient, unknown people built all these mounds."

Downriver and about halfway to Cahokia, we realized the Mississippi River was no longer split into two colors. The Missouri River had changed it from murky green to brown. The Mississippi River wasn't as brown as the Missouri River. Instead, it was a shade of muddy brown. The Missouri River lost its name, but the *murky green was gone*. Herc the Mississippi River narrowed and it appeared deeper and faster.

Hassun briefed us that both the mounds and a Cahokia trading post were on the eastern side of the river. The trading post was farthest downstream and could be seen from the river. The Cahokia mounds' area was more extensive and a few miles inland, while the largest, tallest one was about six miles inland. This great mound was our destination. It provided a bird's eye view of the surrounding area and the river. There was a trail leading to it from the bank. Keme spotted the trail, and we pulled sharply onto a stretch of dry land, fronting a bluff.

Having seen the great mound, Hassun decided to stay with the canoes. The rest of us, led by Keme, scurried up the bank and followed the trail clearly marked by cuts on adjacent trees and footsteps from previous onlookers. Along the way, we passed a few lesser mounds. All were giants compared to our Kickapoo River area knolls. The biggest consisted of several huge mounds heaped on top of each other. It was located on the north end of the Cahokia Mounds collection. For viewing, a small special knoll was on top. It was a long climb to the top, and viewing height was about 100 feet above the river. From here, there was an unobstructed view in all directions. It seemed the original builders had an early warning system in place; their greatest concern was danger from the north. Perhaps their Piasas, a little farther north, were part of that concern.

We couldn't tell with surrounding trees and overgrown areas how many lesser mounds existed. Later we were told by Cahokia traders, "There are more than 100 smaller mounds." An estimate of how many thousand hours of work it took (digging, moving, and stacking dirt and rocks) seems impossible. ***The results were awesome.***

Back on the greatest river in our land, we paddled several more miles downstream and climbed another bank. Directly in front of the trail was a trading post. Next to the trading post was a log church building. This was Cahokia.

Cahokia was controlled by the French, who maintained trade links with traders from as faraway as Canada and the Great Lakes to the north and the Great Sea to the south. They traded animal pelts, food products, and other items including copper, chert, and whelk shells.

Cahokia and Tamarao Tribe villagers related to the Illini Tribe lived in the area. A long-time French catholic priest from Canada built the small church. He converted a number of his Cahokia and Tamarao neighbors.

Greatest Surprise

After a busy, exciting day of meeting the Illinois and Missouri Rivers, Piasa Monsters, and the Cahokia Mounds, a weary group pulled our canoes onto a bank of sand. Darkness was gradually replacing daylight. Though we had food, Keme grabbed his bow and arrows and announced, "It's been a long day, I'll get some fresh meat while you warriors make camp." With that, he climbed the bank and disappeared.

We gathered wood, made a fire, and decided to wait until Keme returned. Game was plentiful, so it shouldn't take him long to make a kill or return empty-handed. We guessed wrong. The Sun was setting, and dark settling, and Keme still hadn't returned.

Chaska and Hassun were climbing the bank to go look for him while I stayed with the fire. Keme came crashing, stumbling, and rolling down the sandy bank to the river's edge. He landed with his butt on the sand and his right foot in the Mississippi River.

Instinctively I ran toward him. "Don't touch me!" Keme screamed, "I'm ruined! A bear killed me in a cane field! I knew those Piasa monsters were black magic. Wisaka made the stunted, stinking French powerful. So there must be something to their belief that confession is good for the soul and preparation for Wisaka's tricky bridge to the Happy Hunting Grounds!"

There was enough light to see his ripped-open left thigh had a large bone exposed and the injured left leg was dangling. His upper body, neck, face, and arms had gashes and claw marks. He was a bloody mess and still bleeding. He had his knife in his right hand. I leaned over to help. He waved his knife and demanded, "Stay away from me! *Just listen, I am going to die; I want to die!"*

In complete shock, we listened to the confession of a self-proclaimed serial killer:

I killed an Iroquois warrior in my fifteenth summer. He was in the woods several miles north of our village. Afraid, I ambushed him;

Next, I killed my mother. I smothered her with a beaver hide. Then made it look like an accident by banging her head on a fireplace rock. It was painful to hear her argue and belittle my father and call us dirty names. She hated everything and everybody. One day I caught Ullich humping her and sucking her right nipple while Father was on a hunting trip where an Illini war party killed him. My manitou wept as we watched mother act like she was overcome with grief. I know she didn't have a chance to confess and is in Hell. By confessing, I hope my manitou will not spend eternity near my mother's manitou;

Everyone knew I could travel like an animal in the woods. Using speed and endurance, I started raping and killing young women. Each time I strangled one, it was like killing Mother again. I felt no remorse. I killed seven girls and two boys who got in the way. The proof is in my medicine pouch.

A burning log collapsed with a muffled crackling sound, creating a huge shower of sparks. In that instant, I saw Keme smiling at me—a weird, proud, kind of condescending smile. He announced, "I was going to kill your rotten sister, but never had the right opportunity." Rolling, he swung his body into the Mississippi River.

Stunned completely out of our minds, we were motionless and speechless. Hassun broke the silence, "Shouldn't we try to save him from drowning?" I heard a voice, my voice screech, ***"No, let the son-of-a-bitch drown. We aren't his French priests, let him go to Hell!"***

Like moths attracted to light, and mindless zombies, we found comfort close to the campfire. Hassun, questioned, "Can you guys tell me what just happened?" I answered, "Chaska and

I found out, and hard to believe, our closest friend has murdered eleven people, including his mother." Chaska added, "Tyr, throw some wood on the fire, and I'll find Keme's medicine pouch."

While I stacked wood on the flickering fire, Chaska and Hassun dragged Keme's canoe next to the fire. Chaska poked around until he found Keme's medicine pouch. Inside was a smaller pouch containing seven small, shriveled pieces of something that could be dried nipples.

Pitch-black dark had arrived, and Hassun kept the fire burning and listened while Chaska and I tried to figure out how Keme could have murdered so many victims without our knowledge or suspicion. We spent considerable time, in-and-out of the woods, with him, and were never the least bit suspicious.

It was common knowledge that Keme could move through the woods like a ghost. He would be gone for several days, having no supervision from parents and very little from others. He usually returned with game he had killed and often shared. We believed he spent those days improving his tracking and hunting skills and helping others.

Neither Chaska nor I had first-hand knowledge of the victims, except the Iroquois warrior, his mother, and the girl killed at a Prairie du Chien trade event.

Achak and Uncle Leno believed that Keme had lied about details surrounding the Iroquois warrior's death. If so, why did he tell a lie? My sister thought he was weird.

Keme was with Mingan and me in the woods when his mother was killed. Or was he? Already tired, we left the village before dark on a planned three-day trip. It was barely dark, when Mingan and I bedded down to sleep. Keme said he was wide awake and would stay up for a while. When we awoke the following day, Keme was with us, and we went on our trip, not knowing his mother was dead. It would have taken luck and wouldn't have been easy. However, he could have returned to the village and killed his mother while Mingan and I slept. Keme and his mother often argued. That wasn't unusual. She found something to argue about with lots of our village people, including my mother. Keme, as far as Chaska or I knew, was never suspected of killing his mother by anyone in the village, certainly not Mingan or myself. We could have been unwilling alibis. Perhaps, he planned it that way.

Chaska and I canoed to Prairie du Chien and were there when the young Menominee girl was murdered. Keme told us that he had sprained his ankle and was staying home. The distance to Prairie du Chien was less than 30 miles by pathways through the bluffs. He easily could have traveled there and slept in the woods away from the crowds. Then found and killed the young girl and returned to the village before we did.

Chaska verbalized his logic: Keme had to be the 'Nipple Savage.' He didn't invent the nipples or the bear; An insane person couldn't concoct such a damming story unless it was true. And they were aiming at something special like saving their manitou for the Happy Hunting Ground; He had to be crazy to believe a confession to us was equal to confessing to a Jesuit Priest; He sounded more like he was bragging than confessing; Remember how I teased him about muscles in his hair affecting his brain? Like when he did some erratic stunt, such as running a 16-foot vertical drop rapid that barely had room for the canoe or touching a giant mama bear. He easily could have killed himself; What if others believe we were involved with the killings because of our close relationship with him? Hassun, having heard the confession, might be the best and only chance of proving our innocence; Also, what will we do with Keme's canoe and belongings? What if his body isn't lost in the Mississippi River, rather it is found by someone who starts asking questions?

My rambling response: What we think we know is a bear badly mauled Keme, and while under great pain and shock,

Keme told us he wanted to die then told an unbelievable, although possibly a true story; In our village, it was known the Nipple Savage killed only four girls. Their manitous are playing in the Happy Hunting Ground and their survivors have long finished their deep mourning; Our actions will not change the past; Knowing his fear of underwater demons, I believe Keme will help us find his battered body; With first light, we should search downstream where with luck we will find and bury his body. Then only tell what we think we know for sure: *Keme was attacked by a bear, died because of his wounds, and we buried him*. That's what we did.

Next morning, within a mile, we found Keme's body facing downstream, caught on a limb and wedged against another tree near the bank of a small island. Keme did want us to find him. He found this dark place where he shoved his knife between upper ribs, and close to his heart. Perhaps he feared an underwater confrontation with the Piasa.

Hassun towed Keme's canoe. It was clumsy work. Before long we had Keme's body and canoe on the eastern bank. Finding a suitable spot, we buried Keme's tortured body with feet pointed west. His personal belongings, including his medicine pouch with contents, were buried with him. We towed Keme's canoe to the next village and gave it to an elderly man. We told him that a bear had killed our friend and we had buried him. The old man thanked us and said, "I am sorry for your loss."

Near term, Keme and his canoe were no longer burdens. Earlier Hassun suggested that he could trade the canoe for something valuable. Chaska and I felt it was wrong to make any trade, and we wanted to close the issue without more questions. Hassan did keep the musket and associated supplies earned by Keme at the Flint River battle. The anguish remained a lifetime burden for the three of us. Keme's confession was one of the saddest experiences and ***the greatest surprise of my life***.

For the next few days, the three of us were in semi-shock and concentrated on floating down the Mississippi River. We briefly stopped at Kaskaskia, about 40 miles south of Cahokia. This French trading post was much like the one at Cahokia. At nightly stops, we continued practicing, handling, and shooting our muskets.

We slowly and painfully accepted that a sick, cunning serial killer had fooled us. For a long time, I felt like a soiled Meskwaki. Later, sadder moments put this one in perspective. Nothing, however, blindsided or surprised me like hearing the first-hand confession of my best friend—**an insane monster**.

About five winters later, a Menominee warrior was caught in the Prairie du Chien area after he killed and sliced off the breast of a young female. He confessed to being THE 'Nipple Savage.' This information took away a nagging worry that something might turn up to challenge our behavior. My belief that Keme was the original 'Nipple Savage' never changed.

Copperheads and the Ohio River

Hassun had never been this far south, so we no longer had the advantage of knowing what lay ahead. A Kaskaskia trader told us, "It's about 150 miles to the confluence of the Ohio River with the Mississippi River and when the Mississippi sharply turns north you will be close to the Ohio River."

Approximately 30 miles farther downstream and near the right bank, we noticed a strange island. It was a tiny, slanted limestone mountain about 20 feet high on one end and 35 feet on the other. It was topped with brush and trees. French priests, extremely convinced and proud of their calling, had painted a big cross on the mountainside.

The shoreside channel was narrow. Still, it was large enough for a canoe. Hassan decided to use the space, so we could see this small, unique mountain up close from different angles. Single file and close together, we squeezed into the channel and found dangerous cross-currents requiring our full attention to steer clear of the mountain island and the rugged bluff on the right. Hassan yelled, "*Look out, **copperheads** on the bluff*!" More than 10 copperheads were napping and two about three footers slithered along a bluff's ledge about eye level and within touching distance. I had never seen a copperhead. It didn't matter; a snake is a snake. Unlike three snake haters and cowards headed south, these two snakes were going north. Thankfully, the encounter was brief. Under Wisaka's guidance, the current quickly swept us past our daytime nightmare. Being in last position, I can verify all paddles were out of the water and aimed at snakes.

Happy to regain the middle of the river, dry and without snake bites. We raised our paddles to the sky in celebration and thanks to Wisaka.

This excitement nudged us back toward the reality and appreciation of being safe and alive. We had no shoreside description of the small unique mountain. Instead, we had an experience that helped dim our shock over Keme's confession.

We knew our meeting with the Ohio River would be soon; how long was a mystery. Early afternoon, we spotted a large sandbar near a small stream. One could swim in the muddy Mississippi. Our preference was cleaner water. To camp near a clear stream, no matter how small, became important. The sun was blisteringly hot, and it would be rare to find a copperhead on a large sandbar, so we called it a day. The following day was another scorcher. Again, early in the day, we spotted a small stream close to a large sandy beach and decided to make camp and go for a swim.

Embedded logs on the far side of the beach were covered with at least 20 sun-soaking, large soft-shelled turtles. Turtle soup would be a nice change from red meat. It didn't take long before six nice-sized turtles, minus shells, heads, and claws were boiling in water from a nearby spring. Gathered greens and spices from our recent rice-boiling Sioux friends were tasty adders to our soft, chewy turtle chunks. Spitting out a few turtle bones was a small sacrifice for a delicious meal. While searching for spices in my canoe, I came across Elyshia's medicine basket. I pulled out the sunflower oil to help protect us from sunburns.

Determined to make it to the Ohio River the next day, we were up at the crack of dawn and on the river by daybreak. Within a few miles, to our amazement, the Mississippi River looped hard from a southern to a northern direction. After about 10 more miles, it looped back to the south. On a much larger scale, the Mississippi River was behaving like our crooked Kickapoo River. Before midmorning, we pulled our canoes onto the small piece of land that separated the Mississippi and Ohio Rivers.

From our embankment view, these two great rivers appeared to touch gently, then peacefully hold hands as they co-mingled a long way to became one. There were some small waves and bubbles. If vicious undercurrents existed, they were hidden from our sight. The Ohio River was wider than the mighty Mississippi River and under the bright sun appeared greenish blue. Downstream the muddy color of the Missouri River prevailed. So, mud from the far west seemed to dictate the color of the Mississippi River.

We decided to paddle up the Ohio River until we were clear of the confluence. There we could catch a few fish, build a fire, cook and eat the fish, and swim in the cleaner Ohio River before resuming our journey. While swimming, we left one hook in the water. A huge catfish took the bait and joined our swimming party. It was more than five feet long and weighed about 100 pounds. Lifting it out of the water, we patted its head and cut the hook from its mouth, then pitched it in the water to grow even larger.

Before pointing our canoes downstream, we were rearranging our loads, when a canoe appeared from upstream and slid in below us. It was an older man with a young guy about our ages. They were both friendly and spoke a language similar to ours. They were *Shawnee* our older brothers. The man's name was Nosh, and the youngster was his son, Noshi.

They had a load of beaver furs and were headed to a French trading post near the Mississippi River's confluence with the Arkansas River. With a little hand-signing, we understood each other. Nosh told us, "We heard the noise and decided to listen before paddling past strangers. You were having so much fun, and your language confused me, so I listened longer than intended. I knew you were nice guys when you took special care of the big catfish." Chaska, our interpreter, was soon talking like a Shawnee and informed Nosh that we were on an adventure to see the Great Sea and had never been this far south.

Nosh noticed our weapons and asked, “Can I pay you to paddle with us for added protection? I have made the trip several times and can help by leading the way.” We promptly responded, telling Nosh that we would enjoy traveling with them and our pay would be just following them all the way.

Nosh replied, “I think this is a lucky day for all of us, because we can help each other. The next 50 miles are a wonderful experience. You guys relax and lead the way. This is a first time adventure for you, so if you want to stop and see something up close, give us a signal. This is Noshi’s second trip and he enjoys stops. After about 50 miles, I will lead the way. The lower Mississippi becomes a crooked mess, and I can help you with the safest paddling techniques. No matter where we are, it’s safer with multiple canoes on the Mississippi River. First, I need to check how much pine gum and birch strips you have for canoe patching.”

He was impressed when we showed him our stash from the Flint River. It didn’t take long before we departed from one of our land’s most important river unions. A scenic wonder, it’s beautiful, calm, and a powerful treasure.

Different Rivers and Incredible Cane Fields

Departing the confluence of two great rivers, we found a changed river. It was wider, a bit slower, with fewer islands, and different scenery. Most of the bluffs and distant mountains were now on the eastern side of the river. Bluffs directly adjacent to the river had been replaced with flood plains contained by low embankments.

The first 50-mile stretch on this changed river was our adventure's most pleasant and relaxed experience. A slight breeze and puffy clouds helped. Seeing distant land adjacent to the river provided a sense of protection against surprises. Too, it was comforting to know Nosh was following us. We didn't see any other people. It was like Wisaka made us temporary owners of this glorious stretch of river and connecting landscape.

Embankments on the western side of *our river* were randomly topped with cane. Stopping between cane fields, we all climbed the embankment. Past the cane fields to the west there was nothing except flood plains sprinkled with relatively new growth. We could see a long way, and no villages were in sight. Nosh told us, "Nobody would build a village in areas consistently flooded by Mother Nature. The cane fields love it. These cane fields have choked out other growth all the way to the Great Sea. Some stretch 100 feet, while others stretch many miles."

This could be very dangerous as already proven by Keme's demise in a much smaller cane field.

Some of these fields and cane stalks were not only large, they were gigantic! We learned they were also important for wildlife. They provided a home and a refuge for black bears, bobcats, cougars, turkeys, rabbits, squirrels, and (Ugh!) rattlesnakes, copperheads, and cottonmouth moccasins. During spring, deer grazed on tender cane shoots. Pigeons and other birds fed on the seeds of the giant cane. All of these creatures didn't live together in peace. No problem; the cane fields were so large there was room for all of them. There was a pecking order on who had first choice, and black bears were at the top.

The cane was useful for many purposes such as: (1) Cooking young shoots as potherb, and gathering ripe seeds to grind into flour for food; (2) Providing material for fuel and candles; (3) Building toys and weapons such as arrow shafts and hunting darts; (4) Weaving baskets for sale and use. There were others too numerous to mention.

Soon this different river changed into yet another river, and Nosh took the lead. He pointed toward a beach, where we stopped and he shared insight regarding what lay ahead:

By river, we are about 1300 miles from the Great Sea and about 600 miles[7] from the French trading post at the confluence with the Arkansas River. The lower Mississippi is largely crooked all the way, with a few straight stretches. The Mississippi River becomes reasonably straight about 100 miles from the Great Sea. The natives call the Great Sea—The Gulf of Mexico;

This trip isn't safe unless you are a strong paddler. One reason I stayed behind the first 50 miles was to find out if you were strong paddlers. There was no tricky paddling required. Still it was obvious you were all strong, careful, and expert paddlers;

All the loose material that gets flushed from the upper Mississippi is called alluvial deposits and is the floor of the lower Mississippi. Early spring flooding from up north, plus southern rains, annually causes lower Mississippi flooding that produces a pattern of alternate bends on the lower Mississippi.

---

[7] The present-day Mississippi River is shorter than it was in the early 1700s.

Two of these bends together look like a regular or reverse ‘S’ and are called a meander. These meanders are easily changed when flooded because their banks cave along the outer sides of the bends;

Rich alluvial soils, and warm humid climates help produce forests of giant hardwoods and cypress. They grow right to the river banks, and their unseen roots can cause damage to boats passing by. A number of trees have caved in and blocked the river, and that’s why pine gum is so important for a canoe in this land; There are many hundreds of meanders in the lower Mississippi. So your journey will require miles and miles of paddling east, west, and even north to progress southward on the Mississippi River;

This is many words one doesn’t have to understand to make the trip. If you follow me closely (several canoes’ lengths) and each following canoe keeps the same distance and takes the direct path of the canoe in front, there will be less canoe patching and we will also be close enough to yell if any problem develops. If there are questions, I will try to answer them.

Chaska asked Nosh, “How many patches have you made on your lower Mississippi trips?” Nosh grinned and replied, “During five trips, about 20 total, and six or seven were made on my first trip.”

Nosh was an excellent leader and knew the river. We followed him as directed, spent a lot of time in the middle of the river, and stayed as far as possible away from big tree roots close to the river bank. Nosh favored different sides of the river depending on our direction, which was constantly changing. We kept the same travel order. Hassan led our group, Chaska, then me. Hassan directly followed Noshi who followed Nosh. It was hard work compared to canoeing down the upper river and required much more concentration. Several eddies spun us around. I was the first one to yell and stop our group for repairs.

Even though we worked very hard we still had plenty of time to kill meat and catch fish, enjoy each others company, plus observe the scenery, and greet the occasional person or groups we encountered.

Approximately 100 miles from the French trading post and floating down the middle of a widened Mississippi River, we saw a group (more than a dozen) of Native Americans on the right bank. Two canoes paddled toward our front and fired a couple of musket balls directly in front of us. Nosh yelled, "They are Chickasaw, we need to answer their fire. They will come after us if we don't fight." Quickly, Hassan put a hole in the bow of the closest canoe, and I put a hole in the bow of the second one, only an inch or so above the water line. Taking on a little water, they quickly headed back to shore. We waved toward the large group, who waved back.

Later, Nosh told us, "I didn't know you guys were sharpshooters. I did figure you could help in case we ran into trouble. And you did! The Chickasaws fight a number of tribes, including the Shawnees and the Quapaws. You will soon meet the Quapaws. The Chickasaws have attacked Shawnee hunting parties near the Ohio and Mississippi River confluence."

French Trading Post and Quapaw Tribe

Several days later, we passed a couple of villages near the Mississippi River's eastern shore. Nosh stood up and waved. Tyr didn't see anybody. Nosh motioned toward the western shore where we beached. I asked, "Who were you waving at?" Grinning, Nosh replied, "I didn't see anybody, they were Quapaw villages, and they saw us. About five more miles on this western shore, we will meet the confluence of the White River.[8] Another few miles, we will meet the confluence of the Arkansas River, also on the western shore. We will need to paddle upstream about 25 miles where the French Post, a very plain structure, is on the right-hand side of the river. There, the French Post's closest neighbor is a large Quapaw village. They are some of the nicest people you will ever meet. If we paddle hard, we should make it by dark. And, my guess is we will all be invited to sleep in their lodges."

We paddled hard, and Nosh's guess became a reality. Along the way, Nosh stopped and pointed to a strange, ugly creature lying in a muddy bayou. He told us that's a 12-foot alligator and we don't plan to get any closer! We had heard of them and learned they only lived in the south.

Before entering the French Post, Nosh beckoned us to gather next to his canoe, where he moved pelts off a sizable container filled with beautiful little pearls. Nosh told us, "Each of these pearls is worth more than all these Beaver pelts. Noshi and I will return to our Ohio country with silver to help our

---

[8] Your storyteller, a river rat, was raised near and on the White River. For centuries the White River emptied directly into the Mississippi River. The Corps of Engineering rerouted the White River, which now joins the Arkansas River before mixing with the Mississippi River.

village. Each of you choose a pearl and hide it in your pouches, to remember this special part of your challenging adventure."

We had nothing of value to give in return. We did make it clear there was no way we could ever forget the friendly expert and son who taught us how to canoe the lower Mississippi River and wished them great futures.

One of the traders came out to see what was happening and greeted Nosh like an old friend. Sundown was near. Nevertheless, there was a lot of activity in the neighboring Quapaw village.

Names at the Trading Post and village have been forgotten. I haven't forgotten how well we were treated and how close the Quapaw village was to a Meskwaki village. Like Meskwakis they grew almost identical foods, hunted many of the same animals, dressed similarly to Meskwakis, and had clans. They built their rectangular lodges the same way, using poles driven into the ground with tops bent over and tied together. They covered their roofs with bark sheets. Like ours, their community buildings were built like lodges only larger. The interiors were like ours. Each village had a chief with an advisory council of male elders, and they had many ceremonies.

Like Nosh predicted, a friend in their village wasn't sleeping on the ground. Nosh was their friend, making us friends, and we each were treated like family.

An important difference is they were great friends with the French and had been since 1673. They wanted peaceful coexistence. They did fight alongside their French troops. The Quapaw's native language was Sioux. Not the same as Chaska's Sioux, although close enough that he could understand many of their words. Nosh, slipped an old well-worn French map of the lower Mississippi in my hands, and told us, "You still have to travel about 600 miles before touching the Great Sea." Anxious to be on the way, we departed for the Great Sea early the next day.

Flying High, Caddo Friends

A decision was made to focus on paddling and gobbling up the distance between us and the Great Sea. Wisaka did us a great favor by introducing Nosh to our group. Nosh taught us how to safely and quickly canoe the meanders. That night we saw the Buck Full Moon, which told us we had been traveling for a month.

For the next 150 miles, we met countless meanders and spent considerable time canoeing east, west and north rather than directly south. Because they were easy to catch and took less time to prepare, we ate more fish. We spent most of our daylight hours paddling toward the Great Sea.

After three days, the 150 miles were history, and we stopped at the confluence of the Yazoo River. Nosh's wrinkled map helped. At least, it showed this was the Yazoo despite no markers or activity. Camping on an inviting sandbar, we left the next morning as soon as daylight allowed. Although our canoe patching stops were fewer and each of us quicker with repairs, the upcoming meanders were dreaded.

Thankfully, there were only a few meanders, and the river straightened for approximately 80 miles. We covered this distance before dark. The following day, meanders were back for another 60 miles. Then the river straightened a little. We encountered more boat traffic (both coming and going). Tired, we bedded down before dark and were up before dawn for another early start.

Traveling almost due south, suddenly, the river made a sharp U-turn: First to the west, then doubling back to the east before slinging us south. Before the southern turn, a small stream flowed into the Mississippi River. Immediately on the eastern side of the river was a stretch of high bluffs. Hassan pulled onto a sliver of sandy beach. We discussed taking a swim in the small, clean feeder stream. Chaska suggested that we climb a bluff and do some high diving before swimming. We needed a break and hadn't high dived (our favorite sport), since Rock River.

Some of the bluffs were about 80 ft. high. It didn't take long to find a place near the small stream where the Mississippi River banged against the bluff, and there was no beach. There was a small beach nearby with a way to climb the bluff. It took about a half-hour of energetic work for all three of us to make sure the water was safe in the landing zones, and there was a safe passage to the bluff's top. As a test, Chaska picked his way to the top and was first to soar from about 70 feet. When landed, he reported, "It's a great clear place to dive from, and there's an audience across the river."

The river was about a half-mile wide, so we didn't notice onlookers. Knowing there were viewers, we decided to give them a show, even though we were rusty. No question Chaska was the best diver and Hassan a close second. Being the biggest and heaviest, I hit the water quicker and made the biggest splashes.

After a couple of showoff diving rounds, a canoe with a young guy (about our age) and an older man named Saku met us at the climbing approach. The man asked, "Do you understand French?" Now routine, Chaska became our spokesperson. Saku came to assure us it would be okay for his nephew to dive with us if it was okay with our group. He added, "My nephew, Delsin is an excellent diver from about 20 feet. Despite pleading for permission, his father (Chief Eagle) has ordered him not to dive off these high bluffs. When you stopped your canoes, none of us knew what you were doing. When it became obvious you were making sure it was safe and we saw you diving like seagulls, Chief Eagle told Delsin, 'If those young men can teach you and say it's safe, then you have my permission to dive from the bluffs.' The chief will pay you well for your help."

Saku and Delsin convinced us with their quiet demeanors and friendly behavior. We agreed to teach Delsin how to high dive for the rest of the day without pay and bring him home before dark. By then, we should know if he has the ability and no fear, just respect, of heights. A pleased Saku departed in his canoe.

Delsin held his right hand up as a friendly gesture, and we followed his lead. He didn't have an ounce of fat on his six-foot body and was about Chaska's age. We started with agility and strength contests on the sandy beach. Then we dove from the beach and a nearby bank to see who could flat dive the farthest and hold their breath the longest. Delsin didn't win a contest. Nevertheless, he was close, competitive, consistent and a joy to work with. His large, strong hands are essential for bluff climbing. He gracefully dived from a 30-ft ledge. Darkness was close, so training ceased. Four tired divers paddled back to the small stream, where all jumped in and had a splashing, great time. Delsin, Chaska, and Hassan did most of the jabbering. Tyr couldn't speak French. By now, I had heard enough that I understood much of the dialogue.

Chaska and Delsin bonded like brothers. Delsin rode in Chaska's canoe, and led the way to his village. There were a few large conical-shaped lodges made with poles covered with thatches of grass.

The weather was pleasant, and we planned to sleep outside. Chief Eagle ordered, "You are welcomed here as family, and family sleeps inside. Tomorrow, before high-dive training, Delsin will show you around, including the coral and horses." Horses! Having never seen a horse, we were anxious to see and touch one.

After the morning meal, Delsin led us to the corral. Chief Eagle's horses were brown with white patches above their noses and ankles. Delsin asked, "Would anyone like to ride one?" Three warriors volunteered. A tame horse was led into a smaller enclosed part of the coral, and Delsin attached a bridle and reins. He explained while demonstrating, "This is what I want you to do." With reins in hand he sprung from the horse's left side, face down, with a rolling motion to its back. Then he lightly tapped his heels to both sides and ordered 'Giddy Up.' He guided the horse around the small corral before announcing 'Whoa' while pulling back on the reins.

Chaska went first and attempted a mount. He made a nice face-down rolling motion starting with his left foot and pulling with his right hand. It wasn't perfect. Still, he ended up sitting squarely on the horse's back. On his first trial trip, Delsin kept the reins and led the horse. On the second round, Chaska held the reins while Delsin held onto the lower right-hand side of the bridle. Then Delsin took his hands off the bridle, stepped away from the horse, and said, 'Go.' Chaska ordered 'Giddy Up' and lightly touched his heels. The horse began moving until Chaska pulled on the reins and ordered 'Whoa.'

Hassan was next, and I went last. All did the same routine well enough and felt with a little training, we could be excellent riders. *Except, the horses wouldn't be very useful in our woodlands.*

Eager to start our 'high-dive training' by midday, we reviewed yesterday's training and showed Delsin climbing techniques and how to minimize climbing risks. He climbed to a 40-ft. ledge and made a spectacular dive.

Chaska stayed about four feet below Delsin during all the climbing exercises and told us when they were ready to go to the top. On Delsin's first high bluff dive, he followed Hassan to the top. Chaska followed Delsin, and I stayed at river level next to the diving target area and watched the three climbers cautiously climb to the top without a hitch. They dove in the same climbing order—Hassan, Delsin, and Chaska. They completed stunning dives and small-splash landings within several feet of each other. Delsin was born to be a high diver!

Chaska told me, "There's a group of Caddos assembled and watching, so we need to put on a show." This was fine with the flyers and me. After we climbed to the top, we decided to dive one at a time, rather than risk the added hazards of group diving. Since I was the biggest, I would go last with a big splash. Clearly, the watchers were entertained.

After two more repetitions of individual dives, we decided to make the next dives our last.

Unfortunately, just above the 40-ft ledge Delsin was using a rock handhold to pull up, and it came loose. The rock and Delsin slipped downward. Fortunately, somehow Chaska caught Delsin, and they were both safe on the ledge. The rock bounced off the side of Chaska's head, leaving a knot and a little blood. Hoping no one saw the close call, Delsin quickly found another handhold, and they went to the top and dove like nothing happened. Chaska had a knot he couldn't hide. Also, Saku and others saw the shortfall. Both Chaska and Delsin were praised, especially Chaska, who may have helped save Delsin from serious injury or death.

Our group spent another night at Chief Eagle's lodge and planned to resume our Great Sea journey the next day. Chief Eagle inspected our canoes and decided they were unsafe to enter the Gulf. He assigned Saku the task of helping their new friends find better canoes and safely make it to the Gulf. Saku was like Uncle Leno—Take charge, learn the details and solve the problems. At first, we protested the extra attention. Saku responded, "Helping you is a small payment for how much you have helped Delsin!" Appreciative, we accepted the help. Saku, had three questions. "What would like to do in the area? How long do you want to stay and how do you plan to return to your village?" By now, it had become automatic that Chaska did all needed translations.

My response was, "Our goal is to see and briefly swim and canoe in the Great Sea. Chaska has a mussel shell full of

Kickapoo River sand to throw into the Sea. We are anxious to leave as soon as our goals are accomplished. We plan to canoe home. If that can't happen we will explore options and walk if necessary."

Saku announced: I will try to help by giving you information and recommendations. First, you were very close to Baton Rouge when diving from the bluff, and we are about 120 curving miles to where the French have completed most of their New Orleans' buildings. From there, it's about 100 relatively straight miles to La Balize, a crude French fort, and the Gulf. You are about 220 miles from your destination. The river speed is approximately three miles per hour. If you paddle hard you can add another four miles per hour. It will take about six or seven days (round-trip) to your Great Sea, named the Gulf of Mexico;

Baton Rouge sets on top of a large plateau that forces the Mississippi River southward. About five miles south of here, the plateau ends, and farther south, the French have a large area where they build, repair, trade, and sell boats of all kinds. For many reasons, it's faster, easier, and safer for three men to paddle one boat rather than three boats more than 1,500 miles upstream. The Frenchman in charge of the boating operation is a good friend. I recommend that Delsin and I lead the way in our boat, called a bateau, and you guys follow to see if we can trade your canoes for one that would satisfy you. The trade should be made before going to the Gulf so you'll have a safe boat.

After discussion amongst three warriors, we ended up with a 24-ft long, five-foot wide, and 26 inches deep canoe—A three-man canoe that was easily handled.

Returning to the Caddo village, everyone seemed happy with our new canoe. We filled it with only belongings we needed and discarded unneeded duplications. Delsin suggested, "Since you have to pass here on your way home, you should lighten your canoe as much as possible, making it even safer for

Gulf handling." Before we finished, Delsin, who had made several trips to the Great Sea and knew a fisherman who kept up with the shifting tides, was leading our group. He and Chaska would lead the way in his bateau while Hassan and I closely followed in the three-man canoe.

This trip would take about six days to paddle back and forth, plus a day at the Great Sea. If trouble happened, it might take longer. Delsin's mother filled some empty space with food and a large container full of special oil for our bodies. The team added fishing tackle and weapons.

Curious about the body oil, Hassan asked Delsin why we needed it? His reply wasn't pleasant information. We learned most of the trip would be in a large swamp loaded with Mosquitos and other pests. The body oil and smoke from our fires did reduce the misery.

Before leaving, Delsin decided to show us something about Baton Rouge that would take a little time. He squeezed us into his bateau and paddled across the river. About a mile past our diving spot, we stopped and climbed a well-traveled trail to the top of the bluff. Nearby, he pointed to a tall red pole and told us, "This 30 ft. red pole was made from cypress and put here by the Houma and Bayou Goula Indian Tribes and served as a marker to divide their hunting grounds. The story goes that about 1699 a French explorer named Pierre d'Ibervill, saw this pole stained red with blood and hanging animal parts and named the place 'le bâton rouge,' I thought you might like to know how Baton Rouge was named." And, we were!

The Great Sea and Homeward Bound

Delsin provided a last minute briefing on what to expect before we started paddling: Your goal to see and swim in the Gulf of Mexico will allow you to see new wildlife and many interesting sights; In ways, it can also be *minor torture.* This time of year, it's hot and very muggy, plus it's our rainy season. Likely, we will be soaked at least once; The 220 miles of river, is about a half-mile wide with nature-made river banks, averaging only a few feet high; Adjacent to the river, on both sides, are miles and miles of swamp or marshland, much of which is at sea level or lower; There are a number of places where the land is high and large enough to hold poor huts that are partly hidden by willows and palmettos infested with alligators and snakes; There are millions of mosquitos, flies, and assorted biting and stinging insects.

A short pause was interrupted by Hassan, who declared, "I'll wait here! Tyr, you can tell me what it's like!"

All laughed. Delsin responded, "Hassan has convinced me. I'll stay with him, and we will practice diving." After a few more wisecracks, we headed to the Great Sea. When pushing off, Delsin's last remark was, "I will tell you about the mud later!"

Besides the Great Sea, New Orleans was another site of major interest. We arrived there on a sunny midday. It was a busy place with people moving up and down the river. Some were climbing a 12 to 15-foot high embankment on the eastern side of the river where New Orleans was being built. Saku had told us, "You will see Canadians, French leaders, troops, craftsmen, Native Americans living in the area, convicts, Blacks, Native American slaves, and a few of our horses."

A French soldier guarded the place to park canoes. He allowed us to climb the embankment with an order to be quick.

We were quick. There were a bunch of rectangular wooden structures made from cypress and pine with workers building them. The pleasant aroma of pine and cypress was everywhere. From this small embankment, one could see miles of flatland in every direction. Lake Pontchartrain was directly north, and in other directions, there were endless miles of swamp, marsh, and muddy badlands. A few Cane Brakes, Bald Cypress, Water Tupelo, and Maple trees watched over these badlands.

Traveling downriver to La Balize, the French fort and the Great Sea, we saw many kinds of wildlife. As part of our scenery, we saw alligators, snakes, big lizards, and lots of frogs. Stopping at a few places, we found worms, snails, insects, rats, clams, crawfish, and shrimp. Plenty of insects found us! Black bears, foxes, armadillos, bobcats, otters, muskrats, beaver, and other animals were in the swamp. We saw our first feral hogs. Their beaver pelts are no match for our woodland pelts. Birds were everywhere, and predators like owls and marsh hawks were on duty. There were bald eagles, herons, spoonbills, woodpeckers, wrens, and pelicans. There were also wading birds like ducks and seagulls whose screaming started at daybreak and didn't cease until dark. They were loud, while their flying and diving antics were treats to behold.

About 25 miles from La Balize, mudflats began replacing the swamps and marshes. Within nine miles of our destination that's about all we could see. The only exception was the Mississippi River had a number of different streams (about five) to the Great Sea. **There was no single mouth.** The French fort at La Balize was the highest point overlooking the Great Sea. It was a sad little fort. We passed more high ground with fishermen's huts before reaching the fort, and arrived about five hours before sundown at Delsin's fisherman friend's hut. He was sorting nets and happy to see Delsin. He spoke the Caddo language and told Delsin, who translated it into French, that we had arrived at a good time. The weather is great, tides are low, you can safely sleep near my hut, the few French men that come and go from the fort could care less about viewers, and fishing is good. Judging by his smiles and enthusiasm, Delsin's friend was happy to see all of us.

Parking our boats below the French fort, there was a hold-your-breath perfect view of the Great Sea that disappeared into the vast horizon. Several fishing boats were in sight.

Chaska was ready with his mussel shell filled with Kickapoo sand. It was time to complete our goals. At first, there was muddy, dirty water for more than a mile. We followed Delsin straight to the clear water of the Great Sea. It was slightly choppy, but there were no problems handling our boats. We steered away from other boats, pulled our two boats together, and held them for Chaska. With no speeches, he simply shook his Kickapoo sand into the Great Sea. We took turns getting into the saltwater, one at a time, while the others held the boats together. We each spent a few minutes swimming, kicking, and playing. It was great fun! Delsin had swum in salt water. For three warriors, this was our first taste of salt while swimming, and we learned how buoyant salt water can be.

Paddling back to shore, we felt like our main goal had been achieved. As usual, Chaska was thinking ahead. He pointed at a sandbar and ordered, "Let's stop here. I'll fill my mussel shell with Great Sea sand and dump it into the Kickapoo." There we were introduced to our first starfishes and lots of crushed pebbles. We each kept a handful of pebbles. Chaska's mussel shell was again a treasure. From our perfect view, we watched an awesome sunset and a sunrise the next morning.

At times, it may have seemed like making the trip wasn't worth the time, trouble, and pain.

The sight, sound, touch, smell, wonder, and mystery of the Great Sea changed our minds! It was worth all the downsides, especially with helpful friends like Delsin, who we met along the way!

Our next goal was reaching Delsin's large conical-shaped lodges near Baton Rouge, which would mean we were homeward bound. Delsin was correct about a measure of torture and he knowingly suffered it for his new friends. We weren't soaked and saw some interesting sights we missed on the trip down. Certainly, we were ***very happy*** to be heading north and away from swamps, marshes, bayous, and mud.

Up the Mississippi River

After the successful return to our Caddo friends' lodge, we stayed the night, and prepared our three-man canoe for the long journey ahead and said our goodbyes to these gracious, giving people.

Saku, the boat expert, suggested that I, being the heaviest, should be in the center of our new canoe. Hassan, the next strongest, should paddle from the back, and Chaska should paddle from the front position. The proper weight distribution would help our speed and take less energy.

Although we were never in danger of turning over, it took more than a few miles after shoving off before we were masters of our canoe. We could talk to each other, which was a tremendous plus. Another plus was our well-trained canoeing muscles. Perhaps the greatest plus was motivation—we wanted to be with our loved ones! It helped to have 12 hours of daylight daily and good weather. *Our focus was on the river, not on scenery or side trips.*

To break the monotony, we did switch canoe positions. Whoever was in the center kept their musket handy. Since we spent many hours near river banks, we could point-blank kill animals for food without hunting. We also fished from our moving canoe.

There was no question that three paddlers in a good three-man canoe were faster than the same three in single canoes. It took less time canoeing from the Great Sea to the confluence of the Ohio and Mississippi River than it took to canoe that same distance down the Mississippi River.

We spent rest days at a few special places, like the confluence of the Mississippi River and Ohio River and the Mississippi River confluence with the Missouri River. A side trip up the Hermit River took a half-day. This was where we spent six days with a special Santee Sioux group, while a rain storm kept us soaked and the Hermit River flooded. When we left, there were still signs of flooding; otherwise, the area was back to normal.

We experienced a number of rain showers both up and down the Mississippi River. Most were little more than nuisances; a few were welcome pleasures.

The differences between our woodland mountain area and the flatland near New Orleans were beyond belief. The closer we were to the Kickapoo River, the harder we tried to paddle. Passing the Flint River, where we became warriors, we only waved. At our campsite later that night, the Green Corn full moon announced: You have been on the Mississippi River for two months; it's time to start a family and get to work.

Rock River village was our next and most important stop. We arrived midmorning. After helping drag the canoe up the bank and parking next to Chepi and Elyshia's lodge, Hassan rushed to his mother's lodge.

Chloe, our hopefully soon-to-be mother-in-law, was the only one home. She was pleased to see us and wasn't surprised when we asked permission to marry her daughters. Chloe asked, "Do you have your parents' approval?" We both replied, "Yes!" Chloe revealed that formality required her to ask the question. Morning Bear and I, along with your parents, conspired more than a little to make this happen. And, we will be pleased to have you as family. The girls talk about you all the time, so I already know their answers.

Chaska asked, "If possible, within a couple of days we need to return home and let our families learn about Keme's death and our safety. We will be back as soon as possible. Our plan is to live here and help support you and the village for a couple of years."

There were no formal ceremonies. We had the needed approvals and *were officially married*. Both Chepi and Elyshia understood our need to return to our Meskwaki Village. All were sorry about Keme's death. Chloe knew most villagers and soon borrowed separate lodges for two nights. The privacy helped make our first days of marriage extra special, and our new wives appreciated their pearls from the Ohio River country.

We left on the third morning with promises of returning as soon as possible. It took four days before we touched the Kickapoo River. Arriving before midday, we stopped where Chaska had picked up the Kickapoo River sand, and he emptied his mussel shell full of Great Sea sand. Together we mixed the sands. Perhaps it was foolish acts, nevertheless it seemed like a good way to end our satisfying and challenging ***Mississippi River Adventure***.

Landing our canoe at the village, we hurried to our respective lodges. Anna, Achak, Uncle Leno, and Grandfather Nodin were home. Others were busy away from the lodge. Anna, with tears in her eyes, said, "Only Wisaka knows how happy we are to see you!" Lots of hugging and laughing followed.

Grandfather Nodin asked, "What were your four most memorable events?" My answers: The first was Chaska and my life changing marriages to Chepi and Elyshia at Rock River; Second, is a terrible memory, Keme was killed by a bear, and I need to let his Uncle Muckki's family know; Third, while at a Mascouten Village on the Flint River, they were attacked by the Illinois. Keme, Chaska, and I were involved. With our silent weapons, we all killed Illinois warriors, so now we are warriors; Fourth, we achieved our goal of seeing the Great Sea and we all had a salty swim.

Achak announced, "Tyr, go share your bad news with Muckki's family. We will have a fire circle this evening and invite others to come. Keme's adventuresome life will be honored. You and Chaska can share a few highlights of your adventure. Our crops are great, so we should have a pleased group of villagers."

The visit with Keme's Uncle Muckki and his wife was short. A bear killed Keme and he had a decent burial was all Muckki needed or wanted to hear. His response, "We are very sorry. Because of the risks Keme kept taking, we were surprised he wasn't killed much earlier."

There was a large, interested crowd at the fire circle. It started a couple of hours before sunset. First, there was a sad memorial service for Keme. Uncomfortably, I provided a few details surrounding his bear mauling death and burial. Chaska and I shared trip highlights and answered questions until about an hour after sunset. We both pointed out how accurate and valuable Uncle Leno's information proved to be. His Mississippi River advice helped us have a successful adventure.

Chaska and I were glad to be home, while the villagers were happy we were safely home, sad about Keme's death, and most were surprised we had married sisters.

Next day, together with our two families, we shared more stories from our Mississippi River adventures and discussed our marriages and near-term plans to live in the Rock River Sauk Village for a couple of years.

In turn, we learned about village changes and the news of relationships with other tribes and our French-Meskwaki peace. A peace that was never peaceable.

A highly troubled Achak told us that Chief Ouchala is now the spokesman for our tribe. He believes it's important to stop ongoing mourning attacks by young Meskwaki warriors and work out an acceptable permanent peace with the French and their allies. Other village chiefs, including me, agreed, and Ouchala is scheduled to meet with Phillip de Vaudreuil, governor-general of New France in Montreal next summer to work out the details of a permanent peace. Unfortunately, chiefs can't control young warriors still eager to avenge their long deceased relatives.

Members of the Meskwaki's Warrior Society (Kiyagamohag) believe they know more than their chiefs and continue to use any reason to kill French allies, especially members of the Illinois Tribe. We will have to wait and see what happens. Chaska, and I did our waiting and worrying from the Rock River Sauk village.

We needed to check our possessions and decide what to take, leave or toss. This didn't take long. It was painful to say rushed goodbyes to relatives and longtime village friends. Most thought, and a few advised us, "You should have delayed your marriages until after returning home. Your action has shown disrespect to your elders."

Chaska and I could have stayed longer. We did make plans to trade visits and keep in touch. We stayed another night. Then, anxious to be with our wives, we departed early the next day.

ELYSHIA AND LATER

ELYSHIA

Chaska and Tyr wasted no time paddling to Rock River. During the trip, we discussed the mountain of unknowns ahead. We were convinced that we had married the right girls and would do our best to have happy, productive lives. Like brothers, we were lucky to be sharing the challenges.

While discussing our wives, we agreed that Elyshia had a strong desire and drive to become a medicine woman, an unusual role for a female. A medicine woman's stature was about the same as a village chief. Chepi, Chaska and me had no goals of equal importance.

There were very few days for the rest of my life that I didn't think of Elyshia. Why? Because she was the most caring, giving, hard-working, loving, and fair-minded person I ever met. Also, she was a precious wife and mother of our children. Again, again and more agains, Wisaka had blessed me.

Chaska and my lives took many unanticipated turns. For example, we didn't go back to our Kickapoo River village after a couple of years. It was 10 years later before I returned to the Meskwaki world.

This was a more peaceful time. Two proud Meskwakis were now living in a Sauk village. Sauks and Meskwakis were good friends. However, Sauks didn't have constant conflicts with other tribes or the French. There wasn't daily discussions about who was killed or constantly worrying about being attacked.

We found our time was better spent. We were warriors defending our village, so we planned and practiced defense that luckily was never needed. Besides family and defense, our most important duties involved hunting, trapping, and fishing. Our village was about 20 miles south of the confluence of the Wapsipinicon and the western side of the Mississippi River. Also, it was about 35 miles north of the confluence of the Iowa and the Mississippi Rivers. Along the banks of these two Iowa rivers were vast prairies filled with game. These were *hunter and trapper paradises!*

Within two weeks of Chaska's and Tyr's Rock River arrival, Hassan traveled to Flint River (where we became warriors) and married his Mascouten sweetheart, Hurit. Then he brought her to live in the village. Hurit, Elyshia, and Chepi soon bonded and became best friends.

Hassan, Chaska, and I had special assignments. For example, the village needed canoe-building help. The Mississippi River adventure team helped build a lot of canoes and a wide assortment of other tasks as assigned by the village chief or council members.

In our third year, the village medicine man became ill and decided to move back to his distant village of origin. He was confident that Elyshia, although very young, was fully prepared to handle the tasks of a medicine man. In addition, her Aunt Kanti was the outstanding nurse. Elyshia, was already loved and known for her medical expertise. She was chosen to be our medicine woman by the unanimous vote of the village chief and council members.

Elyshia was born to be a medicine woman, and she was an outstanding mother. Early summer, during our fourth year, our son, Little Leno, arrived. It was a long trip, back and forth to the Kickapoo River. Despite good intentions, Chaska and I made only a few trips to the Kickapoo River. Our parents made less trips to Rock River.

By Meskwaki tradition, my mother would name her grandchildren. I made a special round trip to bring Anne to Rock

River to name our child. That's how he ended up with the name Little Leno and all our families were pleased.

By this time, Chaska, and Chepi had a two-year-old daughter. Hassan and Hurit had two boys, one three years old and one less than a year old.

Where does the time go when you're busy with loved ones and good friends? Only *Kechi Manitou* knows. Our Meskwaki and Sauk cultures had few serious conflicts, at least that I knew about. One of them is Sauk's call their great God, *Nanabozho, He was involved with the flood and the restoration of Earth.*

Four years later, Elyshia and I were blessed with a beautiful little girl. We spent a lot of happy, loving years at Rock River. Midsummer of 1728, I was leading a hunting party up the Iowa River. We had been there about a week, when Hassan found us and told me, **"Tyr you need to immediately return to the village."**

NO! NO!

All Hassan could tell me was that a French trader had visited our village to discuss fur trapping with a couple of our senior hunters. The Frenchman was sick with a fever, and one of the hunters took him to the medicine lodge for help. Little Leno was in the lodge with Elyshia. Nadi was being taken care of by Chepi at our home lodge.

I later learned that after a close physical examination, Elyshia was convinced the Frenchman had the dreaded disease—***smallpox***. She wasn't certain, so Elyshia put him to sleep and shared her fear with our hunter. Elyshia was determined to take every precaution to keep the disease from spreading. This meant all people who met or were close to the Frenchman or any of his possessions had to be quarantined.

Elyshia ordered the hunter to stand guard and not let anyone enter the healing lodge. She took Little Leno to Chepi, then went directly to the chief and explained the situation. The chief called several of the town council members to a meeting, and this is what she reported: I have never been around smallpox. I did discuss it several times with our medicine man; First, there is no known cure. The initial signs are the victim has a high fever, head or body aches, and sometimes pukes; This Frenchman has all these signs, and he might be contagious; The next smallpox symptom is a rash of red spots. If he has these on his tongue and inside his mouth, they will quickly spread to his arms, legs, hands, and body. These skin sores are filled with a thick fluid. Then puss-filled bumps will appear all over the body that dry and scab over; These scabs start falling off. When the last scab has fallen, the patient is no longer contagious and has lived through hell on Earth; Their reward is a lifetime of scars left on their bodies; The first part of this all happens within a few days. So I should know soon if the Frenchman has it. If he does, the best action for our village is to kill and burn him and all of his belongings; We have no way to monitor this smallpox victim without endangering more of our people. For those who have already come in contact with him, we need to find all of his possessions and burn those as well as his body in a remote spot; All of us who have come in contact with him will not know whether we have caught it from one week to several weeks, during this period we are not contagious. So starting one week from now, all of us that made contact with him or any of his property must be quarantined together away from the rest of the villagers. We must prepare to have another quarantine area for our villagers who have the disease, and we will try to save.

When I arrived at the village, the Frenchman and his belongings were buried ashes. There were two quarantine areas, one for the exposed and one for the villagers, with smallpox. There were three in the smallpox quarantine: The hunter (Nootau) who brought the Frenchman to Elyshia and (**NO! NO!**) **Little Leno** and **Elyshia**. They had been moved to the smallpox victim quarantine only a day earlier. There was a quarantine guard who told me I couldn't enter, and Elyshia begged me to stay away. Little Leno was already so sick he didn't know anyone was there. In profound shock, I wanted to be with my wife and son. The guard knew Elyshia was my wife, and he didn't try to stop me. Elyshia, weeping, fell into my arms.

There is no way to describe the pain, misery, and hopelessness shared and endured by people who love or care for each other while fighting this **monster disease—smallpox!**

Two weeks later Little Leno's scabs started falling, yet he died, and it was now clear that I also had smallpox. Three living adults considered suicide. We didn't have the will or strength to kill ourselves. In some ways, we were happy that Little Leno's manitou would soon be heading to The Happy Hunting Ground. The rules set by Elyshia for villager's smallpox death, required holding the body in the quarantine area for four days. Then when the spirit was free, the body would be treated like the Frenchman—burned and the ashes buried.

One week later, **Elyshia**, my beautiful-wonderful wife, died. At the time, I was too sick to know she was gone.

When most of my scabs had fallen off, and all of Nootau's had fallen, I thought about what kind of rotten God would cause smallpox deaths for two beautiful people while allowing others, far less deserving, to survive.

Uncle Leno had cautioned me, "Tyr, you, and I aren't Gods, so don't try to play God. It's okay to ask for Kehci Manitou's help or mourn if needed. Blaming problems on a God is a waste of time."

The only medical person left in the village was Elyshia's Aunt Kanti, who decided to tack an extra week after all scabs had fallen off before releasing people from the smallpox quarantine area.

My pitted pox scars were so bad they scared my baby daughter, Nadi, making her cringe and cry. After considerable soul searching, Chepi, Chaska, and I decided the best action was for Chepi and Chaska to adopt Nadi. As her babysitter, Chepi had spent as much or more time with Nadi as Elyshia, and no person could provide for and love her more.

I would take a pox-marked body and rejoin my Meskwaki Tribe. It took a while to work out the details, but that's what we did.

Because of Elyshia's knowledge, drive, swift directions, and quarantine actions, she saved many Sauk lives. Only Elyshia, our son, Little Leno, and the French trader died from smallpox.

Greatest Meskwaki Turmoil[9]

My canoe touched a muddy Kickapoo River midday, after the tail end of summer. A bright sun revealed that a recent flood had topped out.

After landing and dragging the canoe through mud close to our family lodge, it was clear—a major flood with loss of crops had occurred, and the village was partly deserted.

An elderly lady, my favorite **Aunt Wapun**, gave me a bear hug and cheerfully greeted, "Tyr, what a nice surprise and welcome to our mess!" Returning the warm hug, I told her that I wasn't sure she would recognize me. She replied, "Once I saw your blue eyes, I knew it was you and you've survived smallpox. Rinse your feet in this big water pot, and let's surprise some more of our family."

Anne, Aunt Nadi, Grandfather Nodin and Uncle Leno were in the lodge. After a round of hugging, I knew this was still home, and Grandfather Nodin hadn't changed much. He ordered an answer, "How did you survive smallpox?"

I described the death of Little Leno and Elyshia; my survival; Elyshia's heroism; Chaska and Chepi adopting my daughter Nadi with my blessing. Now, my goal is to resume being a proud Meskwaki.

---

[9]The detailed names (other than Tyr and his immediate family), dates, locations, and actions described in this section were primarily taken from the book—The Fox Wars (The Mesquakie Challenge to New France) by R. David Edmunds and Joseph L. Peyser; published in 1993 by the University of Oklahoma Press with generous assistance of Edith Gaylord Harper. This fairminded pair of college professors wrote a masterpiece. By far, the best reference book I could find on the Meskwakis for the era covered.

There was a short, awkward silence. Mother Anne, Aunt Nadi and Aunt Wapun responded with condolences and tears. The awkwardness vanished, and I asked, "Where's Achak?"

Uncle Leno answered, "The important question is how can Meskwakis survive? The French and their allied tribes want to **kill all of us** or sell us as slaves. Chief Achak is in another Meskwaki village where a group of chiefs are trying to determine how to save our lives. I think it will take a miracle."

My earlier understanding from Achak was the young members of the Meskwaki's Warrior Society, Kiyagamohag, sporadically continued to kill the French or their allies. We made peace with the Sioux in 1721 and began carrying goods between the French and allied tribes to the Sioux. By 1725, most trades between the French and allies with the Sioux were passing through Meskwaki villages. Even so, Meskwaki conflicts with the French and allied tribes had accelerated far more than expected. My personal problems had left me in a fog.

Achak arrived late afternoon the next day. He was tired, clearly worried, and had information that needed to be shared. He asked us to make contact with all village male adults and tell them, "Chief Achak needs to share important information at the Council Lodge, starting in about one hour. Your attendance is mandatory!" Acknowledging my presence, he hugged me without a word about smallpox, and said, "Tyr, you need to help us spread the word." He heard, "Yes Sir!"

A memory of Achak's presentation follows: **"This is a fact. We are now in our second full-time war with the French and their Native American allies!** Sharing some background information, in 1717, Chief Ouchala emerged as the spokesman for our tribe. During the winter of 1718 and 1719, the Meskwaki Chiefs met in council, and most (including me) agreed our Meskwakis should walk a road of peace with the French and their allies.

"Regrettably, this didn't agree with younger, militant Meskwakis who believed the French and their allies were trying to destroy our tribe. Chief Elecevas and young warriors from his and other villages (including several from our village) continued the path of war, Chief Ouchala admitted to the French that our Meskwaki leadership could not control our young warriors. As you know, Chief Ouchala died last summer. The elderly Chief Okimaouassen is now our primary spokesman. Like Ouchala, Okimaouassen believes our only hope is walking the road of peace because we have no chance of winning a full-scale war against the French and their powerful allies.

"French Governor of New France, Charles de Beauharnois was appointed in 1726. He observed the peace agreements made with Meskwakis in 1716 hadn't worked. In August 1727, Beauharnois secretly decided to kill or sell us as slaves. This initiated the second French and Meskwaki War (1728-1733).

"The major attacks were scheduled to begin this summer. Experience teaches us that grapevines can stretch long distances. The Seneca Tribe of the Iroquois Nation, far to our east and south, learned details about the upcoming French invasion and warned us. Meskwakis and most tribes in the area soon discovered the secret, minus a list of details.

"Beauharnois's army was led by Major Constant le Marchand de Lignery, who left Montreal on June 5 with 400 French soldiers and several hundred Canadian Indians. After major delays, on August 1 they made it to Michilimackinac. There, they were joined by hundreds of Ottawas, Potawatomis, Chippewas, and Hurons. Lignery's total force was about 1,650 men.

"Charles Desliettes, Commander of Fort de Chartres, with his 20 soldiers in Illinois country and several hundred Illinois warriors were supposed to join Lignery's force at the Fox River Meskwaki villages. Near Chicago, they encountered one of our hunting camps and killed 20 Meskwakis and captured 15. The Illinois warriors fought enough Meskwakis for a while and went home. Desliettes thought his 20 soldiers weren't enough to make a difference and reneged on his agreement.

"Lignery's large army seemed to delay at every move, so we had ample time to safely pack food, clothing, and ammunition in leather pouches. Our canoes were readied to carry our women, children, supplies, and evacuate from Fox River villages. In case the French army caught up with us, most of our fighting men followed along the riverbank to provide protection if needed. It wasn't needed. We were long gone toward the west when Lignery crossed Lake Winnebago and entered Meskwaki villages. He arrived August 24, 1728.

"The rapids damaged more than a few of Lignery's canoes. Many of his men weren't appropriately dressed or trained for the difficult terrain. Because of delays their supplies ran low, and they had to eat a lot of corn. His promised support from Charles Desliettes didn't arrive. Some of his Canadian soldiers were reluctant to follow orders, while his tribesmen only wanted to kill Meskwakis. To make matters worse, Lignery was physically sick and refused to delegate authority. He decided to burn the Meskwaki villages and cut down our large fields of corn, peas, and beans. With all his problems, he wasn't sure of challenges past the Fox and Wisconsin Rivers' portage, so there he terminated the mission. His biggest claim for success was, 'My army has starved one-half of the Meskwakis.' Lignery's mission was a complete failure. He and everyone knew it. Beauharnois was highly agitated and recommended Lignery's military rank reduction.

"This is where we are. **Lignery's actions were a gift from Wisaka.** We now know Beauharnois's top priority is to remove Meskwakis from his area of responsibility. Our Fox River Meskwakis are now returning to their burned villages and camping and hunting in nearby forests, so they will have food to last the winter.

"We learned that the Sioux and Ioway chiefs informed the French, 'The Meskwakis can hunt or visit on our side of the Mississippi River. However, we will not allow them to move here.' Thus, if our tribe moves, it can't be west. Your Meskwaki chiefs believe Wisaka **will not** send another Lignery, so Meskwaki life or death decisions need to be made and pursued as soon as possible. In 1712, Meskwaki Chief Oninetonam and his followers departed and stayed with the Seneca Tribe of the Iroquois Nation. We have been invited to join them. At least there we would be dealing with the British rather than the French.

"Evaluating our enemies, the French and allies, includes the Chippewa, Huron, Ottawa, Menominee, Potawatomi, Weas, Illinois, Cahokia, Miami, Peoria, Michagama and Kakaskia Tribes. Our supporting tribes are the Kickapoos, Mascoutens, Sauks and Winnebagos. It's clear that fighting this war is a Meskwaki death invitation.

"We need to continue our regular activities until we decide how to escape. Hopefully, the decisions will be made by next summer. Certainly, we need to defend ourselves. No offensive actions should start from a member of this village without my approval. We need to obtain more ammunition and keep our weapons ready for action. If anything changes, I will let you know as soon as possible."

There was a lengthy open exchange of questions and answers.

For the remainder of 1728 and through mid-1729, our villagers, including me, stayed busy with village needs and activities. We rarely left the Kickapoo River area. I had been absent 10 years. During that time, nine of our lodges were vacated. Most because families felt safer moving to Fox River lodges. Thankfully, we had excellent luck with our trapping and hunting while our fields recovered from the flood.

Our Meskwaki chiefs couldn't agree on a course of action. Unfortunately, or perhaps fortunately, none of them had the power to force the rest of the tribe to do their bidding. The majority of Meskwaki members, like us, went about their work and worried about how and when the French or their allies would strike.

The French were chronic fort builders. One of Charles de Beauharnois's early orders was to build a fort near Lake Pipin. This was on the east side of the Mississippi River about 100 miles north of Prairie du Chien. Of course, the name was Fort Beauharnois. Pierre de Boucherville was the Fort commander, and Father Michel Guignas was the post-Jesuit. After hearing details of Lignery's failures, Boucherville decided to shut Fort Beauharnois down for the winter.

On October 3, Boucherville, Father Guignass, and ten others departed to spend their winter near the confluence of the Illinois and Mississippi Rivers. On October 16, they reached the mouth of Skunk River where they were captured by a party of Kickapoos and Mascoutens and taken to the lodge of Kickapoo Chief Ouiskouba. Boucherville thought he and his party were dead. They were close when a Meskwaki war party of 30 brash young warriors stopped at the Kickapoo Lodge and demanded to take charge to kill Boucherville and his party. Chief Ouiskouba refused, telling our Meskwakis, "We will fight to the death to keep our guests safe." Furious, the Meskwakis stormed out of the lodge and headed toward their village. On the way they encountered two hunters, one a Kickapoo the other a Mascouten. Still angry, the brash Meskwakis butchered and scalped the two hunters and took the scalps to their village.

For Meskwakis, this had terrible repercussions. Both the Mascouten and Kickapoo tribes soon changed their allegiance from Meskwakis to the French. The Winnebagos now believed

Meskwakis were a lost cause, and in the fall of 1729 joined with the Ottawas and Chippewas (around 200 warriors) to make war against the Meskwakis. They attacked an outlying Meskwaki village, killing thirty men and about 70 women and children. Later, this same group attacked a large group of Meskwakis returning from a buffalo hunt, and more Meskwakis were killed or taken captive.

The Sauks were the only tribe left that wasn't making war against Meskwakis. In October 1729, the Winnebagos established a new village on a small island in Little Lake Butte des Morts. Late February1730, the Meskwaki attacked these Winnebagos. This resulted in a siege that lasted until March, 1730. With no winners, the Meskwakis withdrew. Remaining close to our Kickapoo River village, we weren't involved in this siege.

In May 1730, Meskwakis leaders from all the villages assembled on the Fox River in the center of the Mcskawki homeland. We decided to move and live with the Senecas. Any Meskwakis or anyone living with Meskwakis, who wanted to go, were welcome. In our village, all elected to go except nine in Chaska's parents' lodge who moved to a Sioux village located across the Mississippi River from Fort Beauharnois and Uncle Leno. Uncle Leno's reasoning was in addition to his pain, he would require significant help, which would handicap and slow the entire group. He knew the brash young warriors had enough sense to go. This might lead to better treatment for those left behind. Before the end of May, our village members were packed and had moved from our Kickapoo River lodges to the Fox River village that Achak and Anne had moved away from about 36 winters ago. We needed to be closer to the departure area.

Meskwakis sent runners to the Senecas, asking permission to settle in the Iroquois homeland. The Meskwaki runners carried two red stone axes. The Iroquois accepted the axes. They did not offer to help during the 800-mile journey. In early June, approximately 300 men and 600 women and children departed. Wisaka temporarily closed French eyes, so there was no opposition.

The plan was to travel south to the site of La Salle's old fort on the Illinois River, then turn east across the Grand Prairie of the Illinois. Traveling slowly because of the children and elderly, in early July we reached our turning point on the Illinois River. We made a temporary encampment to rest. The elders and children rested while the women repaired clothes and the men hunted meat. Sad to say, a group of Meskwaki hunters met and battled a Cahokia hunting party, who sent runners to nearby Kickapoo and Mascouten villages. Almost unbelievably to us, our brother Kickapoos and good friends the Mascoutens had turned against us. Self-preservation is a strong motivator. We realized the French and their other allies would soon learn about our massive movement.

It was late July when we abandoned our encampment and entered into an endless sea of high prairie grasses, occasionally interrupted by small islands of trees. We headed toward the Wabash River. Despite war chiefs wanting more speed, the heat, humidity, and insect bites exhausted our women, children and elderly. We traveled slowly.

One morning in early August, while fording a small river, we were harassed by a Cahokia war party that had followed us. They were no match for our warriors. We herded our women, children, and elders into a small grove of trees overlooking a river. Our young warriors attacked the Cahokia warriors, who retreated until our warriors came back, then the Cahokias returned. This game continued until afternoon when the Potawatomis, Kickapoos and Mascoutens joined the Cahokias; numbering about 200 warriors. It wasn't a game, my sap buddy, Uncle Etchemin was shot and killed.

We joined our women, children, and elders in the small grove of trees and prepared to defend our families. Both sides traded shots until dark. Seven Meskwakis were killed and 30 wounded. We were trapped and faced a long siege. We had ample supplies of lead and powder. Our hunters had killed several deer and a bison, so those fit went to work to turn this grove of trees into a fortress. No people could work harder than Meskwakis. Three walls were made with the side facing the river left open. The walls were piled-up soil with a wooden palisade on top. The fort was about 150 feet wide and 350 feet long. We filled the fort with small oval-shaped huts, each about three feet wide and six feet long. The hut roofs were reed mats and more piles of dirt.

During a three-week siege, the French-led attackers were joined by nine of their allies—Hurons, Potawatomis, Illinois, Cahokias, Miamis, Weas, Piankashaws, Kickapoos and Mascoutens. A few Sauks were allowed on the French led side, yet helped provide us with some food and saved a small group of Meskwaki children. The French-led group grew to approximately1,400 warriors.

When they realized the hopelessness of their situation, our chiefs offered a number of life-saving options. Following Charles de Beauharnois's orders, the French sensed our endgame was near and absolutely refused any peaceful settlement.

On the storm-darkened night of September eighth, we organized a last-chance breakout. It rained so hard that the French took the recommendation from one of their allies, to not chase us until the storm subsided.

At morning's light, we were exhausted and found ourselves about 12 soaking miles from the fort. I was starving, really weak, and had no dry powder for my musket. Our family was close to the front of the escapees. We passed a little curving creek where I spotted a bunch of willows upstream. I told Aunt

Wapun, who was in front of me, "I'm finished and can't help anyone. I'm going to hide and die." Without answering, she followed. No one else seemed to notice.

I stepped into the creek and waded up a few hundred feet with Aunt Wapun right behind. We drank a little of the creek's water and rested before hearing distant musket firing. This motivated us to keep walking up the briskly running creek, gushing between two high bluffs. The musket sounds grew louder, and screaming and crying sounds like the Meskwaki death songs were heard. We hurried farther upstream. Stepping on a large perch, I caught it. With my knife, we shared a few bites of food. Leaving no tracks, we scrambled at least a half-mile farther upstream, where we found thick willows to hide in, and the creek had surrounded a small pond. We didn't speak until dark, when the sounds were Mother Nature talking. Aunt Wapun was sobbing about the loss of her husband, Etchemin, and the rest of our family. Crying on the inside, I told her, "It sounded bad, but we don't know whether anyone in our family was killed. The clouds are still hiding the stars. I'm comfortable living off the land, so if we're not caught, we will have plenty to eat. Also I'm never totally lost, which means I know the way home. The trick will be, 'Which way is the safest?' Breakfast will be served at daybreak tomorrow and we will decide our next moves."

A small emergency pack tied to my body included line and hooks. The next morning, three nice-sized catfish were hooked and waiting. It was too risky to light a fire. Still, it was a feast that helped rekindle the desire to live. We talked about the safest way home and decided to stay here a few days while most of the French and allies cleared out, then retrace our steps.

Several worrisome moments delayed us. Regardless, Aunt Wapun was an excellent walker, and 21 days later, two unbelievably sad, family friends joined Chief Kiala at his new village on the north bank of the Wisconsin River.

Chief Kiala and approximately 350 others, believing it was Wisaka's will for them to stay in their homeland had elected to remain. Most were older people, women, and children. Chief Kiala felt they could survive if the French accepted their declaration of accommodation.

The Meskwakis, who survived the massacre and eluded capture, were welcomed to Chief Kiala's village. He was desperate for warriors. Unknown by Kiala or members of our new village, Beauharnios met with a Huron Chief and Christian Iroquois who wanted to kill all remaining Meskwakis and gave them his tacit approval. October 17, 1731, 74 Hurons, 47 Iroquois, and four Ottawas headed from Detroit, Michigan to Wisconsin. Their plan was to enlist additional allies before attacking Chief Kiala's village. By the time the expedition had reached the Chicago River, winter had arrived. Trudging on toward the Wisconsin River, the expedition ran into a blizzard that spread snow across southern Wisconsin. About 40 of the party turned back, leaving 50 Hurons and 35 Iroquois, who ran into three Meskwaki warriors tracking a deer.

Beauharnios had earlier promised Kiala that no action would be taken against him before late summer, so we Meskwakis were completely surprised. Kiala's warriors were forced back into our village. When the carnage stopped, 70 Meskwaki warriors and 80 women and children were dead or bleeding in the snow. Additionally, 140 women or children and 14 warriors were taken as captives. Marching their captives toward Detroit, it became apparent our prisoners couldn't maintain the desired pace, so they tomahawked, scalped, and left 56 women, children, and elderly along the trail.

When they arrived in Detroit, the French officer in charge, Jean-Charles Arnaud recommended they kill the remaining captives, which the Hurons and Iroquois were happy to oblige. On learning the results, Beauharnios was so pleased he immediately promoted Jean-Charles Arnaud.

Meanwhile, Chief Kiala and about 15 survivors, including Tyr and Aunt Wapun, made our way to the confluence of the Wisconsin and Mississippi Rivers. Nearby, we found 12 Meskwaki wigwams. Counting, we found remaining Meskwakis had been reduced to about 50 warriors, and 90 women and children.

Aunt Wapun and I backtracked to our nearby Kickapoo River village and discovered it was almost completely burned to the ground. Surprised and shocked, but feeling like trespassers, we didn't even poke around and later learned it had been burned by a small party of Illinois hunters. Chief Kiala and the majority of us decided to return to the old homeland.

As we knew, Meskwakis were vulnerable to any tribe who wanted favors from Beauharnios. We established a small village near 'Lake Maramech' in northeastern Illinois. Chief Kiala and villagers spent the summer of 1732 fortifying our village. We built a blockhouse that served as a watchtower and firing position. Unknown to Chief Kiala or villagers, the Detroit Hurons, with supporting tribes, organized a large war party, and with the blessing of Beauharnios departed in September 1732 to finish the annihilation of Meskwakis. This time scouts brought news of the pending attack, and Chief Kiala and the villagers were prepared and ready to die like Meskwakis if this was Wisaka's will.

Beauharnios's Hurons were joined by the Ottawas and Potawatomis. These two tribes tried to convince Mascoutens to join the venture while the Hurons and a few Ottawas proceeded to our fort. For several days, the Hurons waited for their supporting tribes. When the first attack began, the Mascoutens, Potawatomis, and Ottawas lagged behind and we repulsed the attack, killing a number of Hurons.

Mascoutens, Potawatomis, and Ottawas refused to fight. Potawatomis's Chief Meguesiliguy advised Chief Kiala that now a lot of tribes did not agree with the genocide of

Meskwakis, and that he would try to convince the Huron Chief to agree with a proposed truce. La Forest, the Huron leader, agreed. Mascountens, Potawatomis, and Ottawas eagerly abandoned camp and went home. The sullen Illinois retreated to Lake Peoria, while the resentful Hurons headed back to Detroit.

Chief Kiala spent the winter of 1732-33 huddled around lodge fires with each of us. We were all certain that to stay alive, we needed help from others. The big question was, who? Some suggested renewing our alliances with Kickapoos or Mascountens. After hashing and rehashing options, we agreed that our best hope was living with our peaceful, faithful friends—the Sauks. My testimony about spending 10 years with them helped. In the spring of 1733, we abandoned our Lake Maramech village and sought shelter with the Sauks.

The Sauks with a village on the south bank of the Fox River, at its junction with Green Bay, invited us to live with them. Their village was protected by a palisade and housed more than 150 Sauk warriors. Things went well. The river and nearby bay were full of fish, and the Sauks enjoyed our presence.

In late April 1733, honoring his pledges with the Hurons. Chief Kiala voluntarily surrendered to French Commander Villiers, as a hostage for the continued good conduct of our people. In late June, Villiers delivered Chief Kiala to Governor General Beauharnios in Montreal. Beauharnios ordered Kiala imprisoned in preparation for deportation to the French West Indies, where later, a shackled Kiala and his wife were shipped to Martinique, in the West Indies. Then, still later, they were deported to South America.

Beauharnios also ordered Villiers to assemble a large war party and force all remaining Meskwakis to be delivered to Montreal. If they refused, kill them. Understanding the close Sauk-Meskwaki relationship, Villiers expected trouble. He raised a large war party of Chippewas, Ottawas, and

Menominees. Along with about 60 French traders, the officers and warriors reached Green Bay in mid-September.

We learned they were coming, and retreated into the fortified Sauk village, and prepared for battle. Villiers halted his expedition about a mile from our village. On September 16, 1733, he dispatched about 50 warriors and 10 Frenchmen, led by his eldest son, Ensign Villiers, Jr. to surround the village and block any escape attempts. The rest of the party remained in the camp while Villiers, two other sons, and about 10 other French officers and soldiers proceeded to the stockade gate. The Sauk warriors wouldn't allow the French leader to enter their village and blocked his entrance outside their stockade gate. Villiers verbally repeated the Beauharnios orders and became angry when a quick decision wasn't made. Villiers ordered his outer group, led by Repentigny, to advance and surround the village. Assuming he had frightened the Sauks, he told them to send out the Meskwakis, or he would personally enter the village and get them himself.

The Sauks refused, and Villiers tried to force his way past the gate, and his backup followed. Shots were fired, and one of Villiers's sons fell dead at his feet. Enraged, he fired back, and a general skirmish occurred. A 12-year-old Sauk boy named Black Bird, shot and killed Villier. Responding to the gunfire, Repentigny and troops rapidly advanced forward. They were met by sharpshooting Meskwakis and Sauks, who killed Repentigny and six other Frenchmen, including several more officers. All remaining French forces tried without success to break into the stockade.

There was still panic inside the stockade. Both Sauk and Meskwaki leaders knew Beauharnios and forces would violently react. In the early morning hours of September 19, all the Sauks and Meskwakis abandoned their village and headed up the Fox River. The plan was to cross the Mississippi River and seek sanctuary in Iowa.

Ensign Villiers, Jr., quickly learned of the exodus and mustered the remaining French and allies. They attacked late in the afternoon of September 20, at Little Butte de Morts. Well-armed, the Sauks and Meskwakis were prepared. By nightfall, the Sauk-Meskwaki team had lost about 30 warriors, but killed almost all of the remaining French officers. The Ottawas lost nine, including their chief; the Chippewas count was two killed and several wounded. The French and their allies withdrew to lick their wounds at Green Bay. We continued our exodus and were pleased when the Iowas allowed both our tribes to establish villages in Iowa. We paddled directly to the Wapsipinicon River then turned westward for about 30 miles and established two adjoining, but separate villages.

Since we no longer lived in French territory, this officially ended the second Meskwaki (Fox) French war. Having lived across the river with my wife Elyshia, for 10 years, this was like returning to a special place missing a special Elyshia.

While the war may have officially ended, Beauharnois continued to harass our Meskwaki people, but not the Sauks unless they were directly in the way of an attack. After significant planning, on August 14, 1734 Nicolas-Joseph des Novelles was dispatched from Montreal with a party of 84 French accompanied by approximately 200 Hurons and Christian Iroquois. After a lot of missteps and botched decisions, and killing a few Meskwakis, Novelles gave up. This was late March 1735. It was difficult to change Beaharnois's mind.

However, in June 1738 at Montreal, the Meskwakis officially petitioned Beauharnois for a pardon. Beauharnois granted the pardon and promised there would be no more French harassment of the Meskwakis.

Charles de Beauharnois remained Governor of New France until October 1747. He died in Paris in 1749.

Grace Elyshia Doyle Note

Nadi, daughter of Elyshia and Tyr, born in 1725, married a British fur trader (Lawrence Williams) and moved with him to what is now Cincinnati, Ohio. They had six children. The second, born in 1741, was Kenny Williams, my daddy, who married Abey, our precious mother. She was a Shawnee beauty. They had three children. Born in 1760, I was their second child. The other two were boys who helped make my life interesting. I never understood what daddy did for a living, except it was all about buffalos and bisons. It included buying, selling, trading, and shipping live buffalos-bisons or buffalos-bisons killed by others. English was the language used in our house. Abey was fine with English but insisted we all learn Shawnee to communicate with her family.

Daddy was interested in learning and sharing information about our family roots. Nadi had told him, "My parents were Elyshia and Tyr, whom I never knew because of smallpox. My mother died when I was a baby, and Tyr almost died several times. He was picked up by a tornado and lived, survived smallpox, and as a Meskwaki warrior, had numerous close calls. Fortunately, no one could have had better and more loving parents than Chepi (Elyshia's sister) and Chaska (Chepi's husband and Tyr's best friend), who officially adopted me." Daddy told us, ***"The threads that bind all of us to our past are thin and very frayed."***

My interest in languages grew, and I became an English teacher. I married Connor Doyle (part English and part Irish), who is a land developer. Two years ago (1786), we decided to relocate to St. Louis, Missouri. We had no children, loved the area, bought a house, and Doyle worked fourteen-hour days. I was planning to find a teaching job after I had made the house a home.

There was a French Trading Post, within walking distance from our new house. On my second trip, I saw an old, bent, and scarred Native American holding on to his cane made from cane. I thought, "My God, that could be Tyr." He had a friend with him. I walked up and in English asked, "Are you Tyr?" Puzzled, he pointed a finger at his chest and said, "Tyr." His friend, Wematin, spoke English and told me that he would happily translate words. My first message: "Nadi was my grandmother. Did you know her?" Tyr's answer was, "I did not know her well. She is my daughter." I had to tell him that Nadi died several years ago. I tried my Shawnee and he understood it and responded, "I'm sorry, she was a precious baby." Tyr and his friend were in a hurry to return to their village. They agreed to look me up on their next trip, which they made every two weeks. I gave them directions to my house.

Doyle, a great guy, was pleased that I had found my Great Grandfather. He had no problem with him and his friend visiting. He added, "I don't mind him staying with us. We have plenty of room, and our home for a while will seldom see me and daylight at the same time."

Within a month, I had asked Tyr what he was doing at the village. He answered, "I'm doing my best to be Uncle Leno and help younger guys and girls be the best they can be."

I learned Tyr was amazingly great at recalling memories by rubbing his cane and talking. My daddy's words about memory threads and my writing skills made me ask Tyr if he would like to work with me to produce a written version of his words. He wasn't bashful about anything and loved to talk, talk, talk. He felt like his life had so many ups and downs that it might interest others. **So we went to work!**

Within another month, Wematin brought Tyr and his belongings to our house. Tyr was with us full-time. Doyle and Tyr would wave and smile at each other. Wematin still made his biweekly visit to the French trading post and always visited us to check on Tyr. Sometimes, Wematin helped clear up language problems between Tyr and myself. This process lasted for more than a year when Tyr's health seriously deteriorated and he wanted to die with friends at his Meskwaki village. Wematin took Tyr and belongings back to their village. When Wematin returned two weeks later, he reported that Tyr was in the Happy Hunting Grounds. This was mid October, 1788. My best guess is Tyr was 88 years old.

Several random Tyr thoughts came to my mind: My daddy worked with buffalos and bisons, but I never knew the difference until Tyr explained—buffalos have larger horns and bodies than bisons. Bisons have a hump, larger heads and shaggy coats. Buffalos have smooth coats. More important, bison meat is tenderer and has a lighter, sweeter, and less-gamey flavor.

Tyr often repeated these words:

(1) He was proud to be a Meskwaki;
(2) His role model was Uncle Leno;
(3) He was a defensive warrior, meaning he never went looking to kill anybody. He killed or tried to kill only those attacking him or his family and friends;
(4) The only true friends of the Meskwaki Tribe were the Sauks;
(5) Last but not least, the love and most important person in his life was Elyshia.

Tyr told me, "Great granddaughter Grace, look in the mirror to see a major reason why Elyshia was so important, also I gave up hating the French. Hatred should be a temporary emotion."

Grace Elyshia Williams Doyle

Epilogue

The Kickapoo River is one of the crooked-river champions of America. Cousin Tyr's life was greatly influenced by this unique river surrounded by a panorama of undulating bluffs, hills, and valleys carved out during the last Ice Age.

Tyr's Kickapoo River is still perking along and flooding. Timber cutting, farming, and erosion have added a lot of silt to the river bottoms. It's not the pristine stream it was in the 18th century. Still it's beautiful and interesting enough to be a tourist haven. Wisconsin built Highway 131 to follow the 120-mile Kickapoo from its source to where it empties into the Wisconsin River.

The lack of Meskwaki historical markers along the present-day Kickapoo River is disappointing for one chasing Meskwaki history. Despite France's genocide orders and America's Manifest Destiny policy, today prosperous Meskwakis are very much alive. Considering the tortuous pathway, their long-term settlement in Tama, Iowa, has turned out to be a blessing. ***The Meskwakis have made it a blessing.***

Cousin Tyr would be pleased to learn that many Meskwaki descendants have survived, prospered, and lead productive and happy lives. Perhaps, he wouldn't be so happy about the measure of Meskwaki assimilation into the broader American culture. Assimilate is a nasty, heartbreaking verb for those forced from land they had occupied for centuries.

To deal with the problems of Native American transactions, the Bureau of Indian Affairs (BIA) was established in 1824. The BIA has consistently spent a lot of money, but many of its policies have either failed or created lawsuits and additional chaos. *To be fair, righting past wrongs of governments are almost impossible tasks.*

Loud echoes of that chaos continue today. Helped by failed policies, complicated issues still fester, and many Native

Americans remain mired in a quagmire of federal regulations and despair.

For treaty-making purposes, after the Black Hawk War of 1832, the United States officially combined the Meskwaki and Sauk tribes into a single group naming it the Sac & Fox Confederacy. Through a series of land concessions in 1845, the Sauks and Meskwakis lost (in a fair court today, it would be called stolen) all their lands and were ordered to move to a reservation in Oklahoma. Many were forcibly relocated to Oklahoma. Before the federal shuffling was done, all Sauks and Meskwakis were ordered to reservations in Oklahoma, Kansas, or Nebraska.

Some Meskwakis hid out and remained in Iowa, while others deserted their reservation and, without being caught, returned to their Iowa homeland. This established an unbroken Meskwaki presence in Iowa. Because of their industry, trustworthiness, and friendship with fellow citizens, in 1856, Iowa passed a law allowing the continued residence of the Meskwaki people.

On July 13, 1857, the Meskwakis formally purchased their first 80 acres in Tama County, which gave formal federal identity to the Meskwaki people as the "Sac & Fox in Iowa." Ten years later, in 1867, the United States government allowed the Meskwakis living in Iowa to receive federal annuity payments.

Because the tribe had formed federal recognition and private ownership of their Iowa land, they were in a unique position of unclear jurisdiction and status. For this reason, they received less attention from federal authorities. They used this time to live freer, make sacrifices, and grow. By 1867, the Meskwakis had purchased a total of about 3,000 acres.

Through trapping and accumulating annuity payments, the tribe was able to purchase additional land between 1867 and 1901. During this period, the Meskwaki people were able to live a more independent lifestyle than other tribes confined to regular reservations and strictly regimented by federal authority. ***However, they lived under the constant and serious pressure of the BIA trying to force their return to the Kansas reservation.***

Because their ancestors had the tenacity and intuitive foresight to purchase their land, the Meskwaki Settlement is not a Native American Reservation. It is privately purchased property and a sovereign nation.

In 1987, the Meskwaki purchased additional land toward the north, expanding their holdings to 7,054 acres.

In 1992, the Meskwakis indirectly thumbed their noses at the French of colonial days and others who stood in the way of their beliefs and independence by passing a proclamation that July 13 would henceforth be celebrated as **National Meskwaki Day!** Today, the Meskwakis continue to purchase land as opportunities for economic diversification arise. They currently own more than 8,100 acres of Iowa land in Tama, Marshall and Palo Alto Counties.

The Sac and Fox Tribe in Iowa is the only federally recognized Indian tribe in Iowa. They have their own constitution, codified laws, full-time police officers, and a functioning court system. They have more than 1,450 enrolled tribal members and are the largest employer in Tama County, employing more than 1,200 people.

The Meskwaki Nation has been continuously working to improve housing and infrastructure. They continue to improve modern amenities over the years including beginning their own fiber optic network.

By adapting, surviving, and thriving, *The People of the Red Earth* are working hard to determine the needs within their community. They are committed to protecting their inherent sovereignty, preserving and promoting their culture, and improving the quality of life for future Meskwaki generations.

Meskwakis, like the rest of humanity, are still beset with problems. Nevertheless, considering the obstacles Meskwakis have endured and overcome, their miraculous accomplishments are beyond amazing. Most are now living productive and happy lives while tenaciously clinging to their culture. This is despite big governments (France and America) trying to force them to assimilate into mainstream cultures for more than 500 years. Long term, they have assimilated in common sense ways. A few examples are English is their primary language; They have adapted their business approaches to be organized, friendly, and profitable; Their school system teaches a broader range of subjects and ***they support America*** **if the need arises**.

On August 5, 2022, the Meskwaki Nation held a History of Meskwaki Service Members and reported that 252 Meskwakis have served in the U.S. Armed Forces. This is supporting America!

Pvt. Jonas Poweshiek was probably the first. He enlisted in the U.S. Army June 6, 1917, and was honorably discharged May 1, 1919, He enlisted in Tulsa, Oklahoma, and was identified as a Tama Indian.

After the Japanese attacked Pearl Harbor on December 7, 1941, 27 Iowa Meskwakis volunteered for the U.S. Army. At the time, this was about 16 percent of the tribe's population in Iowa. Eight became code talkers, dangerous and important assignments. These eight were Frank Sanache, Willard Sanache, Dewey Youngbear, Edward Benson, Judy Wayne Wabaunasee, Mike Wayne Wabaunasee, Dewey Roberts, and Mike Twin Sanache, the last surviving Meskwaki code talker, who died in 2004 at age 86.

Those who made the ultimate sacrifice during the Vietnam War included: Sgt. Richard Clive Youngbear, a paratrooper for the U.S. Army who was killed February 3, 1966; PFC Dale Earl Benson, a Code Talker for the U.S. Army, killed

January 15, 1967, and PFC Terry Roberts, a rifleman for the U.S. Marines, killed December 20, 1967.

The Code Talkers Recognition Act of 2008 required Congressional Medals in recognition of the dedication and valor of Native American code talkers to the U.S. Armed Services during World War I and World War II. "Code talkers" refers to those Native Americans who used their tribal languages as a means of secret communication during wartime.

Under the Act, unique gold medals are struck for each Native American tribe that had a member who served as a code talker. Silver duplicate medals are presented to the specific code talkers, their next of kin, or other personal representatives.

On November 20, 2013, at Emancipation Hall in the U.S. Capitol, 33 tribes were recognized for their dedication and valor as Native American code talkers in the U.S. Armed Services during World Wars I and II. Of the tribes recognized, 25 (including the Meskwaki Nation) were presented with their Congressional Gold Medals.

What a Story—The incredible survival of the Meskwakis! These proud, independent, bold, and stubborn keepers of their customs and culture, love their families and Mother Nature. Their ability and willingness to share, work hard, and endure self-sacrifice while suffering endless tribulations is an ***amazingly true and ongoing Saga***.

Miscellaneous Photographs

Captured Meskwakis and Others

This watercolor was by Alexandre de Batz in 1735. He was a French Architect and artist living in New Orleans. This scene is several Illinois tribesmen guarding a small group of captured prisoners. According to research cited by R. David Edmunds and Joseph Peyser, in their book, "The Fox Wars," published in 1993 (photograph by Hillel Burger), the two on the left are a young Meskwaki chief and his wife.

As shown in the next photograph, there were other modes of dress and decorations within tribes and probably villages too. The PD stamp shows this watercolor is old enough to be in the Public Domain.

A Meskwaki Warrior

This watercolor, painted in Quebec about 1730, is also printed in Edmunds and Peyser's book "The Fox Wars." Part of the legend reads: "Fox Warrior. Feared by all nations for their valor and speed, capable of going 60 to 72 miles a day without any food other than plants and leaves from the woods."

The warrior depicted was the Foxes' courier to other nations. He was captured and sent to France, where he died in prison in 1732.

A Group of Meskwaki Leaders

This group helped establish and maintain Meskwaki's presence in Tama, Iowa.

The photograph was taken in 1857

Pvt. Jonas M. Poweshiek
World War 1, U.S. Army
Enlisted June 6, 1917; Honorable Discharge May 1, 1919
(Identified as Tama Indian)

Ely Yang at Wild Cat Mountain Overlook of
The Kickapoo River

Dwain Kitchel at Prairie Du Chien

The Meskwaki and Big Lake Butte Des Morts

The Meskwaki Tribe relocated from Lower Michigan to east central Wisconsin in the early 1600s. They were one of many eastern tribes who migrated westward as a result of the disruptions of the eastern fur trade and the conflicts between the French and British colonies and their various Native American allies.

By 1680 the Meskwaki had established several permanent villages in the middle Fox River Valley. Their grand village, which covered at least 45 acres, was located on high ground south of Big Lake Butte Des Morts.

In 1716, a force of nearly 800 French and their Native American allies attacked the Grand Village of the Meskwaki. After three days of siege, which included the use of cannons, the Meskwaki agreed to a peace treaty, ending the first Meskwaki-French War.

This Memorial is located in Winnebago County, Wisconsin.

Meskwaki Annual Powwow

The Meskwaki Annual Powwow is a four-day celebration held the 2nd full weekend of August each year. The 2022 Powwow was the 106th consecutive year the Meskwakis have shared their way of life. Everyone is Welcome! It's a time of laughter, dancing, singing and reconnecting with friends, family and community. Native Arts & Crafts and History Exhibits are shared with the Food & Fun.

These photographs of young men dancing with families and friends joining in the fun and excitement demonstrate the importance of preserving Meskwaki traditions and sharing customs and cultural awareness.

Meskwaki Nation Day Proclamation Powwow

July 13, 1857 was the historic date that Meskwakis paid $1,000 in gold to purchase their first 80 acres of Tama, Iowa land. The gold was taken to Iowa City and paid directly to Gov. Grimes. Later the Meskwakis passed a proclamation that July 13 would be celebrated in the future as National Meskwaki Day.

The above photos are 2022 participants. At the top, Tiny Tots are competing and the lower photo is the event's honor guard and flag carriers. They are Meskwaki American military veterans who honor the memory of their fallen comrades.

A Winter Concert and Big Laughs

Since January 2020, Felicia Bible has been Music Director at Meskwaki Settlement School (MSS). As shown in the top photo on December 14, 2022, a MSS winter music concert demonstrated significant musical-skill gains. Congratulations Ms. Bible and music students!

During 2022, a group of Meskwaki dads took their daughters to a dance organized by moms. These guys are seated for a surprise game of 'Ring Around the Musical Chairs.' Some would call these 'jokes on us laughs.' A great time was had by most!

Appendix A. History and Timeline of Significant Meskwaki Tribe Events (Early history and Tyr's lifetime)

Before 1614: A precise location of the early Meskwaki Tribe is unknown. It is known that along with more than 30 other tribes, they belonged to the Algonquian language family, collectively spoken by the Anishinabbe people. Anishinabbe tradition believes their earlier ancestors once lived near the Canadian shores of the Atlantic Ocean.

The Anishinabbe people were spread across what is now Canada, the Great Lakes area, and northeastern United States and included such diverse tribes as the Beothuk, Mìkmaq, Delaware, Mohegan, Powhatan, Chippewa, and Meskwaki. The Sauk, Shawnee, and Mascouten tribes (also Anishinabbe people) are all linguistically related to the Meskwaki. Throughout documented history, the Meskwaki and Sauk have stayed in close proximity, often intermarrying. They call each other brothers. Both the Meskwaki and Sauk called the Shawnee and Kickapoo their older brothers.

The earliest known location of the Sauk Tribe is in the St. Lawrence River Valley north of present-day Ontario, Canada and the Meskwakis were farther north near Lake St. Jean.

1614: New Netherlands was established, and the Meskwaki, who now lived near Niagra Falls, New York, began trading with the Dutch, who were located along the Hudson River. Iroquois tribes were also trading with the Dutch and English, who supplied them muskets. The Iroquois Nation of tribes (Cayuga, Mohawk, Oneida, Onandaga and Seneca) were longtime enemies of the French and friends of the English.

Circa 1620: Larger migrations of European colonists began dislodging the northeastern seaboard Native Americans, who pressured tribes to their north and west. To the north, the French were developing their fur trade and were in constant conflict with the English. Trying to survive this pressure, as well as a long-term conflict with the larger Chippewa tribe, the Meskwaki moved southward and closer to Lake Erie.

Circa 1635: With the help of muskets supplied by the British and French, the Huron, Ottawa, Iroquois Nation, and other tribes began displacing weaker tribes, which included the Meskwaki and their brother tribes. As a result, the Meskwaki people became a refugee tribe, retreating past Lake Erie to the present-day Detroit, Michigan area. The Sauks settled north of the Meskwakis at present-day Saginaw, Michigan.

Circa 1642: The Beaver Wars (1640-1701), primarily between the Iroquois and the French and their Huron allies, were being fought. Most Algonquian tribes were soon allied with the French, but not the independent Meskwakis. Heavily armed Iroquois tribes defeated the Hurons and drove the weaker tribes farther west. The Meskwaki, also still under pressure from the Chippewa tribe, once again retreated. Moving west and north, they settled west of Green Bay, close to the present town of New London, Wisconsin. The nearby Winnebago Tribe decided to eliminate their new neighbors. They set out in their canoes on Lake Winnebago with a large surprise war party. The Winnebago warriors encountered a huge storm, and more than 500 of their warriors drowned. Without losing a single warrior, the Meskwakis won a major victory and felt like Kehci Manitou had blessed their settlement.

1665: French traders met a Meskwaki hunting party and asked their name. They answered Fox—their clan name. The French communicated this to the European world. For most of the outside world, even today, Fox became the accepted name of the Meskwaki Tribe. Before year's end, the main Meskwaki group had settled on the Wolf River near present-day Leeman, Wisconsin. The well-fortified settlement of 600 lodges housed more than 2,000 Meskwakis. In addition, they had sizeable hunting camps as far south as northern Illinois and smaller villages along a river that connected Great Lake waterways from Green Bay to the Wisconsin River to the Mississippi River and onto New Orleans. Later, the French named this the Fox River.

Within a year, the Meskwakis and the French developed an uneasy truce, and commenced trading. The French wanted furs; the Meskwaki wanted muskets and implements that made their life easier.

1670: Father Claude Allouez visits the Meskwaki at their fortified stronghold called Ouestatimong on the Wolf River. Father Allouez estimated they had 400 warriors, many who had four to 10 wives. He was aware of the additional and widely dispersed villages and hunting camps. Other estimates were more than 2,000 men, women, and children lived in Ouestatimong. Father Allouez commenced a sustained and failed attempt to convert the Meskwakis to his Jesuit version of the Catholic Religion.

It was about this time when the Chippewa destroyed the last Meskwaki villages on the St. Croix and Chippewa Rivers. Also, Meskwakis made peace with the Iroquois, but still fought the Sioux.

1681: For many years, the Meskwakis had ongoing skirmishes with the Chippewa and Sioux tribes. The Chippewa and Sioux also fought each other. These two large tribes, enraged by the aggression of the Meskwakis, organized a Sioux-Chippewa war party of approximately 800 warriors and attacked Meskwaki settlements in east and central Wisconsin. The Meskwakis withstood the attacks. But 50 of their warriors were killed and several of their women and children were captured. In 1682, the Meskwaki retaliated by attacking a Chippewa village, killing and decapitating several Chippewa warriors and capturing 14 women and children. The stalemate was ended by both sides returning their prisoners.

Late 1680s: Meskwakis began harassing and killing French trappers and traders who used the Fox River to connect with Wisconsin's interior and the Wisconsin and Mississippi Rivers. The Meskwakis, who were no match for the Sioux and large plains tribes west of the Mississippi, were being squeezed on all sides. Tired of retreating and desperate, the Meskwaki felt the French were trespassers on the tribe's river, especially since they were selling muskets to their then enemy–the Sioux. These trespassers could either pay a toll or be killed.

1690: French commander of Green Bay (Nicolas Perrot) enlisted the aid of the Chippewa, and they attacked the Meskwaki village site at the portage between the Fox and Wisconsin Rivers, forcing its abandonment.

1701-1710: In 1701, the French built Fort Pontchartrain at Detroit and began inviting their Native American trading partners to settle nearby. By 1710, approximately 6,000 Native Americans from about 10 tribes had settled near the fort. The Meskwakis were invited, but they were reluctant to be that close to the French fort. The fort was located on land the Meskwaki had settled and held circa 1630. In 1710-1711 approximately 1,000 Meskwakis and some of their Sauk, Kickapoo and Mascouten allies accepted the French offer, and made the journey and built their own fort adjacent to the French fort. Their leaders were Chiefs Lalima, Pemoussa,

Makkathemangoua and Oninetonam. They were unhappy living in the area now controlled by the French and other tribes they disliked and became agitators. The feeling was mutual. It was a tinderbox waiting to be lit.

1712: In early 1712, Makkathemangoua and Oninetonam and their followers departed and joined the Seneca Tribe of the Iroquois Nation.

Potawatomi and Ottawa (French allies) warriors attacked a Mascouten hunting party. The French interfered as the Meskwakis were preparing to help the Mascouten retaliate. The first Meskwaki (Fox) French War (1712-16) erupted. Meskwakis attacked Fort Pontchartrain. The French foiled the attack and began a siege of the Meskwaki's fort, now led only by Meskwaki Chiefs Pemoussa and Lalima. The Meskwakis outnumbered the French and Hurons but couldn't match their firepower. Meskwakis luck ran out with the arrival of 600 additional French allied native warriors. For nineteen days, the Meskwakis withstood the siege. Then during a nighttime thunderstorm, they fled. The French and their allied Native Americans cornered and disarmed them. By the end of the siege and pursuit, approximately 800 Meskwaki, Sauk, and Mascouten men, women, and children were killed. About 500 of those were massacred after the Meskwakis accepted the French offer to surrender if their women and children would be freed and allowed to return to their Wisconsin villages. The French reneged on their offer. Approximately 200 survived and managed to make their way to Wisconsin villages. Chief Pemoussa was one of the escapees.

1713-1715: The scattered Meskwakis staged several revenge raids and ambushes against the French and their Huron, Ottawa, Potawatomi, Illinois, and Miami allies, which paralyzed France's fur trade. The Meskwakis also negotiated a truce with the Sioux and renewed their ties to the Senecas and Iroquois Nation. While the French were deciding what to do in retaliation, Chief Pemoussa consolidated his Wolf and Fox River people into a well-fortified, well-stocked with food and weapons village on a bluff overlooking Lake Butte Des Morts on the upper Fox River.

1716: A French army of 800 soldiers, trappers, and allied tribes led by Louis de La Porte de Louvigny attacked Chief Pemoussa's stronghold. After four days of intense warfare with many casualties on both sides, there was no victor. The Meskwakis agreed to cease their warfare against the French and their allies, and, through the resumption of the fur trade pay, the cost of Louvigny's expedition. They also agreed to furnish six chiefs, including War Chief Pemoussa as hostages to make sure the Meskwakis kept the peace. Under these conditions, the Meskwakis agreed to a peace treaty, ending the first Meskwaki-French War. Chief Pemoussa, and two other hostages contracted smallpox and died. After several years of a fragile-at-best peace, the Meskwaki attacks against the French and allied tribes (especially their hated enemy–the Illini) continued.

1721-1727: The Sioux and Meskwaki, once arch-enemies, decided to become allies against the Illini and frequently attacked them along the Kankakee and Illinois Rivers. During this time the Meskwaki battled their ancient enemy–the Chippewa; also the French and their allied Native Americans.

1728: At the request of the Governor-General of New France, King Louis XV of France ordered the complete extermination of the Meskwaki people. This officially started the Second Meskwaki (Fox) War (1728 - 1733).

1729: A combined Winnebago, Menominee, and Chippewa war party attacked a Meskwaki village killing 80 warriors and capturing 70 women and children. At this point, the Meskwakis realized that most of the area's tribes were now siding with the French. This included their long time allies: The Kickapoo and Mascouten Tribes. Even their Sauk brothers wouldn't fight with them, although they would bring food to their embattled brothers.

1730: About 900 Meskwakis decided their best chance for survival was to leave Wisconsin and accept an offer of sanctuary from the Seneca Tribe (Iroquois Nation) in New York. They chose to pass through Illini country. This angered the Illini, who pursued and caught them on the open prairie near present-day Arrowsmith, Illinois. The Meskwaki built a fort to protect their women and children. The Illini surrounded the fort and sent for help. The help came from many directions, including the French, who took control. After a long siege, the Meskwakis again tried to escape under cover of a late-night thunderstorm. Once again, most were caught, tortured, and killed. A few Meskwakis escaped. Now there were only about 400 scattered Meskwakis left, most in Wisconsin and Iowa.

1733-1738: The remaining Meskwakis sought refuge with the Sauk tribe. The French thought allied Algonquian tribes would finish the extermination without French help. The Meskwakis continued their successful and long-enduring alliance with their brothers (the Sauks) and tenaciously endured until the French decided it was in their best interest to rescind the genocide order.

1754: French Indian War (1754 -1763) was the fourth and final series of conflicts in the French and Indian Wars. Again, as expected, Meskwakis, while few in numbers, were allies of the British and helped wage war against the French.

1763: The British were victors of the French and Indian War, which ended the New France colony. The remaining Meskwakis and Iroquois people must have been almost as pleased as the British. This was also the year of the outbreak of Pontiac's War (1763–1766). Native American tribes resisted British settlement of the Great Lakes region.

1775-1783: *The War of American Independence*. While still a very minor factor, the Meskwakis continued to support the British. They feared the aggressive, land-grabbing colonists more than the British, who previously had been their ally against the French. During this time, General Washington, Commander of the Continental Army, waged a campaign against the Iroquois Seneca people in the New York area who supported the British and who, at the time, were friends of the Meskwaki. Washington obliterated more than 30 Seneca towns. Many were killed, and their towns and crops were burned to the ground. The survivors fled to Canada. The Native American name for George Washington was *'**Town Destroyer**.'*

1784-1794: After Washington was elected America's first president, he understood there was significant Native American resistance left to overcome, and one never knew when another European army might attack the new country. Washington convinced the new congress that a standing army was needed. There was much congressional opposition because the ragtag colonial regiments from the 13 separate colonies, under Washington's overall command and with the help of the French had defeated the British. The first official general of an American Army, General Anthony Wayne, was appointed by Washington in early 1792.

Timeline Post Script:

2023: Here we are, approximately 335 million Americans whose welcoming monument is still the Statue of Liberty, donated by the French in 1875 as recognition of their support and help during America's Revolutionary War, then later were America's staunch allies in two World Wars. In 1883, Emma Lazarus wrote her famous words:

Give me your tired, your poor,
Your huddled masses yearning to breathe free.
The wretched refuse of your teeming shore.
Send these, the homeless, tempest-tost to me,
I lift my lamp beside the golden door!

America opened the golden front door in 1886, long after we had pushed most Native Americans out the back door. At first, this back door was the western banks of the Mississippi River. Later, it included the rest of America. Native American land was stolen with cheap goods, alcohol or false promises. Then they were isolated on reservations located on the least valuable land of the times, chased into Canada or Mexico, or were killed.

European diseases were, mostly unintended, major factors in the total death count. Native American death by disease was welcomed by many Americans (including Presidents Andrew Jackson and Teddy Roosevelt) who believed it was their **Manifest Destiny** to clear the land or isolate Native Americans.

Included in this 335 million are now about 5 million Native American survivors. Population-wise, that's about the number in 1500 when there were few white people or other groups in North America. Now, in America, Native Americans are surrounded by 330 million people from about every country and ethnic group on the planet.

Thanks in measure to approximately 500 years of failed American policies, many Native Americans are still trapped in their reservations and suffocating federal regulations that other citizens don't face, including millions of legal and illegal immigrants (whose number is conservatively estimated to be 12 million–more than double the number of Native Americans). Meanwhile, the number of illegal immigrants, thanks to failed federal government policies, continues to steadily increase.

Appendix B. The Vikings and Native Americans

Viking Early History

The northwestern region of the Roman Empire was populated by Norsemen. Like our earliest Native Americans, they were primarily hunters and gatherers living in nomadic bands with no written records. By 476 A.D., the western part of the Roman Empire was no longer controlled by the Romans. At about this time, Norsemen began farming the land and using the North Seas for fishing and commerce.

Viking is an old Norse verb for an overseas expedition. It traditionally meant taking time during their summers to go 'a Viking.' This eventually involved raiding as well as legitimate commerce and exploration. *The Anglo-Saxon Chronicles*, in a 787 A.D. entry written by English scribes, reported the first known record of a Viking attack, "Came first three ships of the Norsemen from the land of robbers. The local sheriff then rode to the shore to meet them; for he knew not what they were; and there was he slain."[10]

An increasing Norseman population, with their warlike nature, shipbuilding and sailing prowess, created a subculture that terrorized Europe for several centuries. That subculture was called **The Vikings**. Most came from the Scandinavian countries, now commonly referred to as Denmark, Norway, and Sweden. Few could have predicted this small, fierce group, with their limited resources, could dramatically impact and influence the World. Against all odds, they did!

---

[10]In 2008, two complete Viking ships were uncovered at Salme, Estonia. Archeologist's analysis of the ship's contents show that Viking attacks were initiated approximately 50 years sooner than the recorded 787A.D. attack.

Out of the northern mists, in 793 A.D., they savaged St. Cuthbert's Church, one of the holiest and richest shrines in the British Isles, spattering it with the blood of the priests, despoiling its ornaments, and taking its riches. From that date until 829 A.D., the Vikings conducted hundreds of brutal attacks. One positive factor was they only went "a viking" during the summer. Then gathered their loot and returned to their homeland, allowing their potential victims to relax and breathe easier during the fall, winter, and spring.

Starting about 830 A.D., they changed tactics. The number of their murderous attacks increased to include all seasons of a year, as did the size of their raiding parties. Typical Viking fleets grew to 35 ships, and in the following decades, some had more than 100 vessels. They also began to build fortified coastal bases and occupied and settled the lands of their conquests. For more than 150 years the Vikings raided, plundered, raped, and killed Europeans almost at will. In 899 A.D., England's Edward the Elder began the first successful campaigns against the Vikings.

During 830-954 A.D., the Vikings expanded their trading partners to include Russia, Slavic countries, Spain, Constantinople, Morocco, and others. They also mingled and intermarried with those they conquered or met, especially Orkney and Shetland Islands occupants. A 2014 DNA study[11] by the English found that only 3 percent of Britain's population had Nordic DNA. In contrast more than 25% of Orkney and Shetland Island residents had Nordic DNA. The same study found an insignificant amount of Roman DNA in Great Britain's citizenry. It is like the Romans were never there. The last major attempt at a Viking hurrah came in 1066 A.D. when Viking

---

[11] Study by Britains DNA organization, Dr. Jim Wilson, chief scientist, using only paternal linkage. Many British citizens were surprised the Nordic DNA percentage was so low.

King Harald Sigurdsson invaded England with about 270 ships and more than 10,000 soldiers. He was soundly defeated and killed by England's King Harold. Many historians choose 1066 A.D. as the end of the **Viking Age**. This doesn't mean the Vikings disappeared. Rather they were no longer feared as a dominant, significant force because so many had been killed or assimilated by other cultures.

Vikings in Iceland and Greenland

Here, our primary interest is in the Viking's westward expansion and contact with North American Natives.

Viking sailors discovered Iceland, and Norsemen began settling there in 870 A.D. During 982 A.D., Erik Thorvaldsson (Erik the Red), a Viking chieftain who resided in Norway was convicted of killing several neighbors in an ongoing feud and was banished to the Iceland colony for three years as punishment.

Erik sailed with his wife, three sons, and daughter to Iceland, where he spent the next three years. How do we know this? We don't. It's better to ask, "Why can we believe this?" The basis of this belief is a collection of Viking stories (called Sagas), written by Icelandic priests in the 13th and 14th centuries, describing the life of Viking Icelanders and Greenlanders. These Sagas were based on hand-me-down oral legends. For centuries most reputable historians dismissed the Sagas as nothing more than entertaining tales or myths with perhaps some measure of truth. Two of these Sagas (*The Saga of the Greenlanders* and *The Saga of Erik the Red)* are the basis for the following information.

Erik the Red, during his banishment, sailed the uncharted sea west of Iceland and discovered land. He found several sites that were attractive for settlement. After his banishment period ended, Erik, a man of action, recruited a large number of pioneer families to settle his new colony. He named it Greenland. In 986 A.D., Erik headed back to Greenland with 25 Viking longships and hundreds of settlers. Only 14 ships successfully made the voyage. Erik established two settlements, which eventually housed about 3,000 people. One settlement was on the southern tip of Greenland and the second was on Greenland's southwestern coast. These settlements flourished and lasted more than 300 years before failing. This has been confirmed by archeological evidence. Putting that time in context, it lasted longer than America's current existence (1783 to 2023).

Of the 11 longships that didn't reach Greenland, 10 either returned to Iceland or were lost. Bjarni Herjolfsson was blown off course while sailing from Iceland to Greenland. He continued sailing westward and finally sighted land on a coastal area surrounded by forests. This clearly wasn't Greenland with its fjords and mountains. Keeping land on his left in sight, Bjarni steered his ship in a northerly direction for a couple of weeks when, at last, he found and joined the colony.

Since Greenland lacked an abundant supply of timber, Bjarni's description of a heavily wooded land located a couple of weeks by longship southwest of Greenland was potentially useful. One of those most interested was Erik the Red's son, Lief. Leif was unable to make use of this information for fifteen years. During that period, he served as a leader-in-training at the Viking court of Norway's King Olaf, married Thorgunna, had a son named Thorkel and converted to Christianity.

Vinland

Returning to his father's realm in Greenland, Leif renewed his acquaintance with Bjarni Herjolfsson. He bought Bjarni's longship, and with Bjarni and a crew of 35 cast off and sailed south to locate the land of large trees. This was in the summer of about 1002 A.D. Retracing Bjarni's earlier course,

Leif came to a place he called Helluland (land of flat rocks). Continuing south along the coast, Leif encountered a heavily forested area where he made landfall and named it Markland (land of woods).

Curious and with little fear of the unknown, Leif resumed sailing south. Within a few days he steered his longship into a wide harbor surrounded by grassy land that, in turn, was adjacent to verdant forests. After Tyrkir, a crew member, found vines with grapes, Leif named the area Vinland and established a base camp. There he and his crew built sod huts and spent a mild winter. During this mild winter, they built larger housing and explored the land farther south along the coast. Seafood and game were easily accessible. They filled their longship with wood and grapes in early spring and returned to Greenland.

Leif's father, Erik the Red, soon died, and Leif became Greenland's chieftain. While his duties kept him in Greenland, he retained ownership of the Vinland base camp and was involved in future expeditions to the area.

About1004 A.D. a second expedition returned to the base camp in Vinland. This expedition with a crew of 30 was led by Leif's brother Thorvald. Their mission was to conduct more exploration and bring back another shipload of wood. They survived the first winter by fishing. In the spring and summer, they explored west and south and encountered no signs of humans except for one corn shed. They spent another winter at the base camp. The following summer Thorvald encountered some small natives they called Skraelings (barbarians). On the sandy shore, they saw three skin boats with three Skraelings under each. Thorvald's men killed all except one, who managed to escape. Revenge for their murderous actions was quick. They were attacked by a large number of Skraelings. Arrows killed Thorvald and a couple other crew members. Then the Skraelings retreated into the forest. His crew buried their dead and later returned to Greenland.

Thorstein, brother of Leif and Thorvald, decided to bring his dead brother back to Greenland for a proper burial. He and his wife, Gudrid, set sail for Vinland's base camp with a 25-man crew. After sailing a good part of the summer without finding his brother's remains, Thorstein returned to Greenland.

During the following winter, Thorstein died of an illness. That same winter Thorfinn Karlsefni arrived at Greenland from Norway and married Gudrid (Thorstein's widow). Karlsefni agreed to lead another expedition to Vinland. There's confusion between Sagas on the size and number of people involved in Karlsefni's expedition. It is estimated that he had three ships and a crew of about 150—135 men and fifteen women. His new wife went with him. Since they planned to settle there for a while, they brought along a herd of cows and a bull. Finding the base camp in good shape, they stayed there for the winter.

The following summer, a group of Skraelings visited the base camp. They brought skins to trade. They wanted weapons in exchange but settled for ribbons, red cloth, and milk. Early the next winter, the Skraelings returned with more skins to trade. One of the Skraelings tried to steal a weapon and was killed by a Viking. The other Skraelings scattered into the forest. Karlsefni assumed the Skraelings would return in large numbers for revenge. He was right. Karlsefni and his Viking crew were prepared and killed a number of the Skraelings before the natives abandoned the fight and retreated into the woods. This ended trading with the Skraelings. Karlsefni stayed another winter before returning to Greenland.

About 1009 A.D., a fourth and final recorded Viking expedition to Vinland occurred. It was a doozy. Leif's stepsister Freydis and her husband Thorvald planned a trip to Vinland. Two brothers (Helgi and Finnbogi and no kin to Freydis) had recently arrived in Greenland from Iceland, and their ship was larger than Thorvald's ship. Freydis decided that she wanted the brothers to join them on the expedition. The brothers accepted the invitation. The two ships put to sea, and both safely arrived in Vinland. Freydis's ship had a crew of 35 men and five women. The brothers' ship had a crew of 30 men and five women.

Skipping most of the drama and intrigue that ensued, Freydis convinced her husband and crew members to kill the brothers and their crew members, which they did. However, they refused to murder the five women. Freydis took an axe from one of the squeamish men and proceeded to kill each of the women. The murders took place during the winter. When spring arrived, the murderers loaded up the brothers' ship and returned with their cargo to Greenland. Their collective and rehearsed story was, "We left the two brothers and their crew alive and well in Vinland. They will return later." Leif later learned of their evil actions but refused to punish Freydis. He did prophesy that her descendants would never thrive and supposedly that came to be.

The above expedition descriptions came from *The Saga of the Greenlanders*. *The Saga of Erik the Red* corroborates much of the information. But there are some variations. For example, *The Saga of Erik the Red* account consolidated the expeditions into two expeditions instead of five and they worked from two base camps. The first was Vinland. The second was south of Vinland and named "Lot."

Both sagas show that during the first decade of the eleventh century, more than 160 Vikings traveled to Vinland. Some stayed for a couple of years. While in Vinland, they spent a significant amount of their time exploring.

L'Anse aux Meadows

In the early 1950s, Helge Ingstad, a Norwegian explorer and author, began a focused quest to find Vinland. With the aid of the Viking sagas and an ancient Icelandic map, he searched thousands of miles of the North Atlantic coast, looking for signs of Vinland. He lost count of the blind alleys and his many disappointments. Finally, in 1960 he heard about some ruins near a fishing village named L'Anse aux Meadows. The village was located on the northern tip of present-day Canada's Newfoundland.

When Helge first saw the area, he thought, "Of 'meadows,' which is the same as 'grasslands' in Nordic . . . just what Norsemen were looking for." He soon met George Decker, a lifetime resident of L'Anse aux Meadows. Mr. Decker directed him to a site west of the village. There, a number of mounds were overgrown with bushes and tall grass. Unbelievably, these mounds had been clearly visible for more than 900 years. The villagers believed Native Americans had built the mounds. They called the location, "The Old Indian Camp." Mr. Decker informed Ingstad that no one had ever dug there.

Helge's wife, Anne Stine, was a Norwegian archeologist. After they were married, she became his scientific collaborator and companion in exploration adventures. Anne and their daughter, Benedicte, were with Helge when he first toured the L'Anse aux Meadows area.

Over the next seven years, in cooperation with Parks Canada, and under the leadership of Anne Helge, the site was excavated. Outlines of eight structures with sizable walls were found. The structures' styles were Viking. So early on, the Helges felt they had found Vinland. It took a lot more than feelings to prove it. After four years of meticulous digging and weighing the evidence, in 1964, they found a Norse spindle-whorl, used throughout Scandinavia in a device that spun wool into yarn. They now had irrefutable proof that linked the site to Norsemen. ***Vinland had been found***. Or was it found? No question, it proved the Vikings were in North American almost 500 years before Columbus and 1492. In 2009, the Norse settlement at L'Anse aux Meadows was dated to approximately

1,000 years ago (carbon dating estimate 990–1050 CE), an assessment that agrees with the relative dating of artifact and structure types

There are many researchers and historians who believe L'Anse aux Meadows was just a settlement on the northern perimeter of Vinland.[12] They believe this settlement was used as a base for exploring. The dig findings showed no evidence or effort to make L'Anse aux Meadows a permanent settlement. Thus one can reason that Vinland must include land to the south. Land located as far away as present day Maine or perhaps even farther. **If** ever found, that site will probably be referred to as "Lot" as described in *The Saga of Erik the Red* account.

So, Who Were the Skraelings?

Based on L'Anse aux Meadows' geographical location, the Skraelings whom the Vikings first encountered were likely either the Beothuk or Inuit or both. The Skraelings were keenly interested in red cloth and traded furs to the Vikings for this material.

Beothuks migrated from Labrador to the Island of Newfoundland about one A.D. Scholars have estimated there were 700 to 2,000 Beothuks when many European contacts were first made at the beginning of the sixteenth century.

They lived in independent, self-sufficient family groups of about 40 people with group leaders that weren't called chiefs. During spring, the Beothuk used red ochre to paint their bodies,

---

[12] Dr. Annette Kolodny, teacher, historian, and author is one of those who believe only a temporary settlement in Vinland has been found. Her book, *In Search of First Contact, The Vikings of Vinland, the Peoples of the Dawnland and the Anglo-American Anxiety of Discovery* is a first-hand, comprehensive collection of information and insightful analysis of the Viking presence in North America.

canoes, and almost everything they owned. They were known as "Red Indians." For them, the use of red ochre had great cultural significance, and it designated tribal identity. A form of Beothuk punishment was not allowing a tribe member to wear red ochre colored adornments.

The Beothuk people were reclusive, basically keeping to themselves. There are records of intermarriage with Mi̇kmaqs, who also considered themselves "Red Earth People." Unlike neighboring Indian tribes, the Beothuks didn't have an interest in acquiring muskets.

For reasons such as loss of access to important food sources, competition with Mi̇kmaqs and European settlers, infectious diseases and violent encounters with trappers and others, the Beothuk people are classified as extinct. Shanawdithit, the last known Beothuk, died in St. Johns, Newfoundland, in 1829.

Mi̇kmaqs also migrated from the north and lived in Newfoundland, later they moved into Nova Scotia and New Brunswick. Their hunting parties still crossed the Cabot Strait and competed with the Beothuk for game and seafood in Newfoundland.

Beginning about 1500 A.D., contact between Native Americans (the Wabanki People) and European sailors became routine. Basque, Spanish, French, British, and Irish fishing boats visited the Grand Banks each summer. By 1519 the fishermen were coming ashore to dry their catches and trade with Native Americans, who had long told of ancient encounters with 'dangerous people who came from the north.' Arrows were said to bounce off their skins, and these strangers were described as having 'no human sympathies.'

The Wabanki tribe members were also called the People of the Dawnlight. Their tribes were located along the Atlantic Coast and first to see the sun each day. The confederacy included the Mi̇kmaq, Maliseet, Passamaquoddy, Abenaki and Penobscot tribes.

Mìkmaq mothers and grandmothers in New Brunswick, Canada sometimes tell their blue-eyed children they are Viking descendants. Among the Wabanki tribes, there are many reports of 'first pale-face sightings' that have been passed down orally. They may be reliable. Also, they could be caused by closer to 1500 A.D. contacts rather than a Viking first contact.

Dr. Kilodny's exhaustive efforts to sort fact from fiction of oral first contact reports between Native Americans and Europeans led her to conclude, "In the twenty-first century, to recover among Native peoples any reliable trace memory of a contact that occurred 1,000 years in the past is like following a will-o'-the-wisp, that faint, elusive light that sometimes plays at night over marshy grounds. At best, there are hints, tantalizing clues, and conjectures. Even what appears at first, as hard evidence turns out to be subject to conflicting interpretations. Yet stories about some first contacts—or first sightings—have endured."

Meskwaki Tribe

Two tribes that called themselves "Red Earth People" were the Mìkmaq and Meskwaki. Both belong to the Algonquian linguistic group. The red Indian Beothuks also spoke a variant form of the Algonquian language.

The Mìkmaq spiritual concept of a great manitou, with lesser manitous for anything else, agrees with the Meskwaki spiritual understanding.

Tyr's paternal grandparent's repeated recitation that his distant ancestors had sex with pale-faced, blue-eyed Vikings may be a stretch, but is certainly possible.

A better understanding of Viking and Native American relationships depends primarily on three factors: (1) Additional archeological evidence, (2) Improvements in DNA testing and analysis accuracy and (3) Substantially more Native American and Nordic DNA tests.

Bibliography

Cousin Tyr Text and Appendix A

Armstrong, Perry A., *The Piasa: Or, The Devil Among the Indians*, E. B. Fletcher, printer, 1887.

Bronowski, J., *The Ascent of Man*, Little, Brown and Company, Boston/Toronto, 1973.

Brown, Richard Frank, *A Social History of the Mesquakie Indians, 1800-1963*, Iowa State University, Iowa, 1964.

Billard, Jules B., Editor, *The World of the American Indian*, National Geographic Society, 1974.

Carter, Cecile Elkins, *Caddo Indians, Where We Come From*, University of Oklahoma Press, 1995.

Cassidy, James J., Project Editor, *Through Indian Eyes*, The Readers Digest Association, 1995.

Deboe, Angie, *A History of the Indians of the United States*, University of Oklahoma Press, 1983.

Eckert, Allan W., *The Frontiersmen*, Jesse Stuart Foundation, Ashland, Kentucky, 2001.

Edmunds, R. David and Peyser, Joseph L., *The Fox Wars*, University of Oklahoma Press, 1993.

Forsyth, Thomas, *An Account of the Manners and Customs of the Sauk and Fox Nations of Indian Traditions*, 1827.

Harris, Eddy L., *Mississippi Solo, A River Quest*, Henry Holt and Company, New York, 1988.

Hogeland, William, *Autumn of the Black Snake*, Farrar, Straus and Giroux, New York, New York, 2017.

Jones, William, *Ethnography of the Fox Indians,* Smithsonian Institution, 1939.

Kellogg, Louise Phelps, *The French Regime in Wisconsin and the Northwest,* State Historical Society of Wisconsin, Madison, Wisconsin, 1925.

Mann, Charles C., *1491, New Revelations of the Americas Before Columbus*, Vantage Books, New York, New York, 2006.

Marsico, Katie, *The Mississippi River*, Cherry Lake Publishing, Ann Arbor, Michigan, 2013.

McTaggart, Fred, *Wolf That I Am: In Search of the Red Earth People,* Reprint, University of Oklahoma Press, 1984.

McHugh, Tom, *The Time of the Buffalo*, University of Nebraska Press, 1972.

Murphy, Lucy Eldersveld, *A Gathering of Rivers*, University of Nebraska Press, 2000.

Paterek, Josephine, *Encyclopedia of American Indian Costumes*, W. Norton & Company, 1994.

Payment, Simon, *La Salle, Claiming the Mississippi River for France*, The Rosen Publishing Company, New York, New York, 2004.

Riley, Naomi Schaefer, *The New Trail of Tears, How Washington is Destroying American Indians,* Encounter Books, New York, London, 2016.

Robertson, Marion, *Red Earth Tales of the Mi'kmaq*, Nimbus Publishing LTD, 1969, 2006.

Ruthhart, Roger, Internet, rruthhart@qconline.com, 2011.

Scanlan, Peter L., *Prairie du Chien*, George Banta Publishing Company, 1937.

Schneider, Paul, *Old Man River*, Henry Holt and Company, New York, 2013.

Sheltrone, Henry Clyde, *The Mound-Builders*, The University of Alabama Press, 2004.

Shimer, Porter, *Healing Secrets of the Native Americans*, Black Dog & Leventhal Publishers, Inc. New York, New York, 2004.

Starr, D. Barry, Ph. D., *A Handy Guide to Ancestry and Relationship DNA Tests*, Stanford University, 2017.

Steinmetz, Brad, La Farge: *The story of a Kickapoo River Town*, Kickapoogian Press, 2010.

Sultzman, Lee, *Sauk and Fox History*, First Nations Histories, http://www.tolasga.org, 2017.

Tall Bear, Kim, *Native American DNA: Tribal Belonging and the False Promise of Genetic Science*, 2013.

Taylor, Alan, *American Colonies, The Penquin History of the United States,* Penquin USA Books Group, NY, NY, 2002.

Taylor, Colin E., *The American Indian*, Courage Books, 2002.

Tedlock, Barbara, *The Woman in the Shaman's Body*, Bantum Dell, Random House, Inc., NY, NY, 2005.

Warren, William W., *History of the Objibways*, Based Upon Traditions and Oral Statements, Minnesota Historical Society, St. Paul, 1885.

Washburn, Wilcomb E., *The Indian in America*, Harper Torch Books, 1975.

Yenne, Bill, *The Encyclopedia of North American Indian Tribes,* Crown Publishers Inc., 1986.

Young Bear, Ray A., *Manifestation Wolverine, The Collected Poetry of Ray Young Bear, Open Road Integrated Media, Inc.,* New York, New York, 2015.

Appendix B The Vikings and Native Americans

Brown, Dale M., *The Fate of Greenland's Vikings*, Archaeology Magazine, 2000.

Ingstad, Helge, *The Viking Discovery of America*, Breakwater Books, Ltd., 2000.

Kindrick, T.D., *A History of the Vikings*, Charles Scribner's Sons, 1933.

Kolodny, Annette, *In Search of First Contact, The Vikings of Vinland, the Peoples of the Dawnland and the Anglo-American Anxiety of Discovery*, Duke University Press, 2012.

McDonald, R. Andrew and Somerville, Angus, *The Viking Age*, University of Toronto Press, 2010.

Pringle, Heather, *New Visions of the Vikings*, National Geographic, Vol. 231, No. 3, March 2017.

Reeves, Authur M., North Beamish & Rasmus Anderson, *Norse Discovery of America*, Amazon Digital Services, 2010.

Sephton, J., *The Saga of Erik the Red,1880 Translation to English.*

Somerville, Angus A. and McDonald, R. Andrew, *The Viking Age,* University of Toronto Press, 2010.

Starr, D. Barry, *A Handy Guide to Ancestry and Relationship DNA Tests*, Self Published, Stanford University, 2017.